WEST

NORTH

SOUTH

EAST

Graveyard

PARKING

Corn Crib

Dry House

Summer Kitchen (Seasonal)

West Family Wash House

Preserve Shop

West Family Sisters' Shop

West Family Dwelling

Public Rest Rooms

Old Stone Shop

Carpenters' Shop (Craft Store)

West Family Privy

Old Ministry's Shop

Slate House

Farm Deacon's Shop

Medic Garden

Orchard

Carriage House

Meeting House

Ministry's Workshop

Centre Family Dwelling

Water House

Brethren's Bath House

East Family Brethren's Shop

Coopers' Shop

East Family Dwelling

Shaker Life Exhibit

East Family Sisters' Shop

East Family Wash House

Historic Farm

Dining & Lodging

Trustees Office (Dining Room and Lodging Registration)

Post Office (Craft Store)

Administration Building

Village Entrance

To West Lot — Hiking and Horseback Riding Trails

US 68 to Harrodsburg (7 miles)

US 33 to Lexington (24 miles)

US 33 to Danville

Danville (13 miles)

1.7 miles to Riverboat

1 mile to Riverboat

Timber Frame Stable

Shaker Landing

RESTORING
SHAKERTOWN

RESTORING SHAKERTOWN

The Struggle to Save the Historic Shaker Village of Pleasant Hill

THOMAS PARRISH

❧

FOREWORD BY
THOMAS D. CLARK

❧

AFTERWORD BY AL SMITH

THE UNIVERSITY PRESS OF KENTUCKY

Publication of this volume was made possible in part
by a grant from the National Endowment for the Humanities.

Published by The University Press of Kentucky
Scholarly publisher for the Commonwealth,
serving Bellarmine University, Berea College, Centre College of Kentucky,
Eastern Kentucky University, The Filson Historical Society, Georgetown College,
Kentucky Historical Society, Kentucky State University, Morehead State University,
Murray State University, Northern Kentucky University, Transylvania University,
University of Kentucky, University of Louisville, and Western Kentucky University.
All rights reserved.

Editorial and Sales Offices: The University Press of Kentucky
663 South Limestone Street, Lexington, Kentucky 40508–4008
www.kentuckypress.com

09 08 07 06   5 4 3 2

Library of Congress Cataloging-in-Publication Data
Parrish, Thomas (Thomas D.)
   Restoring Shakertown : the struggle to save the historic Shaker village of Pleasant Hill /
Thomas Parrish ; foreword by Thomas D. Clark ; afterword by Al Smith.
     p. cm.
   Includes bibliographical references and index.
   ISBN 0-8131-2364-X (hardcover : alk. paper)
   1. Historic buildings—Conservation and restoration—Kentucky—Pleasant Hill. 2.
Historic preservation—Kentucky—Pleasant Hill. 3. Pleasant Hill (Ky.)—Buildings,
structures, etc. 4. Shakers—Kentucky—Pleasant Hill—History. 5. Pleasant Hill (Ky.)—
History. I. Title.
   F459.P555P37 2005
   363.6'9'09769485—dc22   2005018027
   ISBN 978-0-8131-2364-6

Manufactured in the United States of America.

Member of the Association of
American University Presses

Contents

Illustrations follow page 82

Foreword

Rebirth of a Historic Community

THOMAS D. CLARK

❧

T ucked away safely atop a shoulder of the Kentucky River Palisades, Shakertown at Pleasant Hill in Mercer County, Kentucky, near Lexington, is one of the best preserved and managed of the communal sites in North America. It is a national treasure—twenty-nine hundred acres of beautiful land and restored buildings that was once a thriving village created in the nineteenth century by believers of a curious religious sect committed to the practice of communal, but celibate, living. This book tells how the village was saved from the ravages of time and neglect and became an impressive landmark in the historic preservation movement of the second half of the twentieth century.

But first, a word about the origin of the Pleasant Hill Shaker community. With more than a dash of folk wisdom and foresight, northern emissaries of the socio-religious mystic Mother Ann Lee came to Kentucky in search of converts two hundred years ago and located a modest beginning site on the winding Shawnee Run Creek, a lateral of the Kentucky River. By 1808 the village was moved up ridge to a knoll to be called Pleasant Hill.

In a frenetic moment when Kentucky was aglow with religious revivalistic fervor, wandering Shaker proselytizers found it relatively easy to recruit members for their Society of Believers. At Pleasant Hill they planted a self-sustaining religio-agrarian foothold. Well outside the pale of the religious fundamentalists, the discipline and order of Mother Ann was based upon a strong element of Quakerism, the Established Church of her native England, and a generous outpouring of mysticism.

The order grew in numbers, to a zenith of five hundred in 1830, the third largest of the nineteen Shaker communities then in America. There came experienced farmers, herdsmen, craftsmen, food processors, and skilled marketers. Standing above the rank and file of converts was the gifted Virginia youth Micajah Burnett, a self-taught architect and builder who planned and oversaw the construction of a cluster of remarkable buildings of an adaptive Georgian style. No Kentucky builder ever used native Kentucky materials to so graceful a purpose. Burnett's remains lie in an unmarked grave of the village where he labored, but his genius is remembered in the high degree of perpetuity he assured the structures at Pleasant Hill.

Their craftsmen unable to compete against an expanding commercial-industrial economy, their beliefs undermined by a waning of religious enthusiasm and a weakening of their faith in celibacy as the nineteenth century moved forward, the Shakers slowly succumbed to the blight of worldliness in changing times. With the death of the last surviving Shaker, Sister Mary Settles, in 1923, the village was returned to "the world."

In recounting how Shakertown was reassembled as an outdoor museum in the second half of the last century, the largest restored Shaker community in the country, Thomas Parrish has presented a fascinating chronicle of the village's evolving fortunes. He deals effectively with the challenges of financing, of finding the best preservation experts, and of following their advice to achieve the highest standards of authenticity possible. In terms of management, his story credits, properly, the enormous contribution of Earl D. Wallace, the longtime chairman of the restoration effort; but he also includes the criticisms of those who objected to what they saw as Wallace's attempts in the last years of his leadership to move the mission from historic preservation to conferencing—primarily annual meetings on socioeconomic issues conducted by the Shakertown Roundtable—while ignoring suggestions for further work on the infrastructure at Shakertown. Toward the conclusion of this story, it will be apparent that Wallace's successors as chairmen redirected the program, and

substantial fund-raising, toward the preservation mission. But adherence
to preservation as a central mission, however admirable, has not exempted
Shakertown from a decline in visitor attendance that has been noted at
historic sites all over the United States in the first decade of a new century.
I would suggest that Shakertown trustees may want to revisit mission issues
yet again.

Personally, I saw Shakertown for the first time in mid-summer, 1929.
It stood as a proud but sadly deteriorating roadside Kentucky settlement,
and seemed to be growing shabbier daily. Over the next three decades restoration was only a vapid dream of a few concerned individuals. When
Wallace came along, as a retired oil executive turned Wall Street financier,
he was at the right juncture of life and profession to give full attention to
the restoration challenge that Thomas Parrish describes. He was also so
newly pastured from New York that the passion of financial pursuits was
still upon him. He exulted in the quest for money to make the restoration
a reality.

Without him, as one trustee said, there probably "would have been no
restored Pleasant Hill Village." But it is also true that Wallace, who became
one of my closest friends, seemed never to have had more than a passing
interest in the Shakers' spiritual affairs or their socioeconomic order. He
was about as far away from being fascinated with turning or grazing the soil
as a man could be—but he did lust, in the words of that ancient maxim,
"for the adjoining land," and it drove him, spurred on by James Cogar,
until his last breath, to reacquire for Shakertown nearly three-fourths of
the four thousand acres once owned by the Believers.

But Wallace was only one individual in the down-to-earth restoration
of the crumbling, inside and out, physical remains of Shakerism. The talent of James Cogar is stamped, figuratively, on every board and brick in the
village. Cogar's special knowledge of antiquities was beyond anything Wallace
had ever conceived. James Thomas, a young staff addition recruited by Cogar,
came aboard already seasoned in preservation work in Louisville. Restoring
and refurnishing the interiors of the building became a monumental task.
For over forty years of service at Shakertown, from assistant to James Cogar
all the way up to president and then chief executive officer, Thomas remained faithful to two guiding principles: authenticity and integrity.

While Parrish has drawn the saga of restoration efforts by leaders, trustees, and dedicated staff into a comprehensive whole, the question remains: How does the restored Shakertown fit into the rapidly changing environment of the twenty-first century? There is little doubt that a tourist visit to Shakertown is a pleasant experience. But what obligation endures to preserve the *spirit* of the Shakers when they were striving to better the conditions of humanity? How should the successful salvage of their physical community be used to present the rise and fall of the Shakers' dream of protected, self-sufficient isolation on the American frontier?

Private gifts, magnificent and generous as they were, did not save Shakertown alone. The Commonwealth of Kentucky gave vitally needed support; so did the American people through the largest federal loan of its kind, at the time, for historic preservation. While historic preservation was indeed central to the purpose of both private and public assistance, it may be argued that giving the public a forum for public discussion of vital issues, as Wallace urged, is not an inappropriate dividend for the public and private investments made. Nor is it all that distant from the Shakers' search for better answers to questions of peace, justice, and harmony between humans and the God of nature.

Although Parrish chronicles the tensions that developed over Wallace's support of a roundtable to probe a multiplicity of socioeconomic issues, he also indicates that the neglect of infrastructure needs charged to Wallace in his old age has been addressed. This should clear the way for a reconsideration of the roundtable role by those who are now responsible for Shakertown's future. It seems to me that in its great beauty and tranquil setting as a retreat from the nineteenth-century world, Pleasant Hill has the potential to be a major national site, a middle ground in the heart of the country for public discussions about the problems of the world, and the future of the world in the twenty-first century.

Since Wallace's death in 1990, a dynamic trio of leaders—William T. Young, Alex Campbell, and James Thomas—have shepherded major physical advancements to the point that never in its modern history has Shakertown enjoyed such a pristine condition. The dream of Edenic American beginnings is preserved in its broad green acres of pastoral land enclosed in long rows of rock fences sheltering the handsomely restored village.

Symbolically, this is a community, like a bride in gown and veil, awaiting a suitor who will accompany her happily to a new level of purpose of life itself.

Thomas Parrish's book is not only an objective revelation of the struggle to restore Pleasant Hill Village. It is a handbook to be read carefully by all dreamers across the land who set out to reclaim the past by resurrecting its monuments. Surely those of the past, Mother Ann Lee, Elder Rufus Bryant, Micajah Burnett, Earl Wallace, Jim Cogar, William T. Young, and all the faithful will sing a gentle Shaker hymn approving of this book.

—Thomas D. Clark

Thomas D. Clark, who died in July 2005 at age 101, was Historian Laureate of Kentucky for Life and Professor Emeritus of History at the University of Kentucky. The many books he authored include, with F. Gerald Ham, *Pleasant Hill and Its Shakers* (Pleasant Hill, Ky.: Shakertown Press, 1968).

Preface

✤

O ne spring afternoon a companion and I visited the Shaker Village of Pleasant Hill, a National Historic Site in the Bluegrass country of Kentucky, some twenty-five miles southwest of Lexington. We lunched in one of the dining rooms in the building known as the Trustees' Office—being sure to top off the meal with the famous Shaker lemon pie—and then, with other visitors, spent the next two hours following an archaeologist from nearby Centre College as he moved through the village, telling us details about the buildings we could see and showing us sites on which lost buildings had stood.

Our ad hoc group then followed him down a mile-long road, a former twentieth-century state highway that had been turned back into the macadam road of earlier years, to the partially excavated site of a mill that sat by the watercourse called Shawnee Run. The archaeologist explained how, with their well-known ingenuity, the builders had taken power from this small stream to operate a sawmill, a gristmill, a linseed oil mill, and a fulling mill; they had also woven woolens here. As we listened to our guide and looked around the little valley, all of us, I think, imagined that we could see Shakers in costume hard at work at their various tasks.

The afternoon was balmy, but with a sky of almost autumnal blue, and as we walked back up the road to the village, we marveled not only at the great inventiveness of the Shakers but at their perfect taste. They had created a world of simple beauty and serenity, a jewel in a green setting, with the curves of the landscape and the clean lines of the buildings coming together in perfect harmony. Half a mile away cars moved on the relocated state highway, but they were external, not really intruding on our scene.

Everybody in the group asked the leader questions about the Shakers and their works and about the preservation of their village. I had questions, too, but I had my own special purpose in asking them and, indeed, in being there that day. I was going to tell the story of the rescue of the village from decay—how and why it was preserved, and who the people were who did it, and what kind of time and effort the task had required—what obstacles these people had overcome and what kinds of ingenuity they had, in their time, drawn upon. I thought it would turn out to be a good story, and it did.

A ny book is the product of a collaboration; without the aid of a variety of helpers, the person who is officially the author would achieve little. Hence I wish to express thanks to the many willing volunteers and also—though this is a book written for a general and not an academic audience—to give credit to printed and other inanimate sources as well. Readers wishing to go further into one or another aspect of the subject will find some suggestions for that in the sources and background, page 159.

I also wish to make special acknowledgment of the cooperation and help of James Thomas, Brenda Roseman, and the staff at Pleasant Hill, and I thank my friend Al Smith, who conceived of the project and boldly undertook to serve as my editor. Happily, we remain friends.

CHAPTER I

"That Wonderful Village"

❦

Back in the 1950s, Jimmie Campbell, an engineering student at the University of Kentucky, used to drive regularly from Lexington down U.S. Highway 68 to visit his sister in Danville. He became thoroughly acquainted on these trips with every curve on that narrow road, including the series of tight turns dropping down to the Kentucky River at the Jessamine-Mercer county line and its counterpart series across the river, climbing up again and onto the rolling Mercer County plateau. A few miles farther on from the river, Campbell would come to a special landmark on his forty-mile drive—a low stone fence, in need of some repairs but distinctive nevertheless, that marked the beginning of the lands surrounding the most unusual village in the entire Central Kentucky area— the old settlement called Shakertown, after the members of the remarkable religious sect that had established it early in the nineteenth century. A 1904 guidebook to the Bluegrass spoke of the village as "the home of the most peculiar people on the face of the globe."

Approaching the village itself, young Campbell would pass a large square building on his left that seemed to be serving as a silo, stuffed with hay. Then, knowing the road, he would slow down a bit because a sharp curve would put him right in the village. Driving past several big brick and stone buildings—"all of them looked like boxes"—he would pass, on the left, one that was used as an inn. He never stopped there. Although he went on to have a distinguished career as a civil servant in Lexington (including, on his retirement, having a street named after him), his budget in those days had little room, he said, for eating at restaurants. For Campbell, Shakertown was, at best, a place to get an occasional few gallons of gas at the little Shell station.

Apparently he missed quite a dining adventure; another visitor to Shakertown in that era enjoyed better luck. Dick DeCamp, who spent a good bit of time in Lexington in the late 1950s and moved to the city in 1960, recalled that he and his friends "all used to go down to Shakertown and eat when the Renfrews ran the restaurant. The place had a lot of character. It was like something out of a Faulkner novel, going there for dinner. They just had some tables around and the old shades were on the windows." It was a bring-your-own-bottle operation, DeCamp said, and the food was wonderful. "They just had a few things—a special eggplant casserole and fried chicken and old ham, but they'd never get it ready." Guests would sit out on the front steps and "kill a bottle of whiskey," and finally a member of the party would stroll back into the kitchen and casually ask, "How're things coming, Mrs. Renfrew?" The lady would look up at her interlocutor from her cup of tea, "but it wasn't tea." Finally everybody would get fed, and then somebody would wind up the old Victrola in the corner and put on a record, and sometimes a waitress would join in the dancing. Those who, like Jimmie Campbell, just drove through Shakertown had no idea of the delights they were missing.

DeCamp also remembered the filling station, with its old-style pumps out front. It was in one of the larger old buildings that also housed a country store. A frame building along the street, between the inn and the general store, bore the sign: SHAKERTOWN BAPTIST CHURCH. One of the buildings was painted "a hideous brown," one observer said, and a number of the others were covered with fake red brick paper. Some of them had porches and lean-tos that obviously had been added long after the original construction. Old cars sprawled outside a repair shop, and the Shaker graveyard presented a thicket of cane and brush. Banks of wires stretched between utility poles, and advertising signs hung from some of the buildings.

The village of Shakertown may have had its gustatory charms, but all in all, as one woman said, "it was not much of an inspiring sight." Looking at it in 1959 or 1960, you seemed to see just another Waco, as in Madison County, or Little Rock, as in Bourbon County, or Salvisa, as in Mercer County—except for those big buildings. For however it may have looked, Shakertown was not a typical Kentucky farm village. Behind the buildings lining Highway 68—those unusual buildings doing ordinary duty as the inn and the church and the general store—stood others, large buildings of stone and brick, many of them boarded up, some dilapidated but others seeming eminently sound, thanks to their obviously solid construction. That, together with their location close to a well-traveled highway, probably accounted for their having survived weather and vandalism through the years relatively intact, solid evidence of a past far greater than the present. "Where nineteenth-century travelers on horseback had been startled by such immense structures," one writer observed, "twentieth-century motorists passed by and wondered at the incongruous buildings." In a way, Shakertown, a village sitting in the shadow of an earlier civilization, resembled a Karnak or a Troy with a pair of Shell pumps. "You could get a sense of what it had been," one person remembered, "and what it could be."

"There was always much talk," said DeCamp, "about 'what's going to happen to that wonderful village?'"—the wonderful village lying beneath the humdrum, commercial, twentieth-century surface. Such talk had been heard, one way or another, for more than forty years. Shakertown had ceased functioning as a religious community in 1910, and just a few years later an exotic story had spread through the area. It seemed that the newly founded House of David, a religious group as out of the ordinary as the Shakers, had expressed interest in buying Pleasant Hill, which the members apparently considered a suitable spot in which to await the establishment of the Kingdom of God on earth, an event believed to be imminent. But nothing came of this possibility, or of the prophecy, and the House of David went on to win its greatest renown in the years between the world wars as the sponsor of a traveling baseball team each of whose members, in a decidedly clean-shaven era, sported a flowing beard.

During the Depression, talk was heard of turning Pleasant Hill into a state park, but that led nowhere either. Meanwhile, the last of the local Shakers had died, and a Harrodsburg businessman that had acquired the rights to the village and the surrounding farmlands sold the property at auction. The buildings changed hands many times during the ensuing decades, and from time to time in the 1940s and 1950s people discussed the possibility of restoring the village. In 1960, six persons owned the buildings in the village, with the neighboring farms in the hands of five owners.

Shortly after the end of World War II, Burwell Marshall, a Louisville lawyer who owned some of the buildings, had formed plans to open the village for visitors, but he and two brothers, George and Herbert Gwinn, who held most of the farmland surrounding the village, could never reach an agreement on a right-of-way to bring water from the pumping station across the farms and to the village itself. The Gwinns, however, had made an important contribution to the area in the realm of land conservation. By the time the Pleasant Hill community was dissolved in 1910, the land had suffered from long neglect, with orchards abandoned, rock fences tumbled, and topsoil in many places washed away "down to the clay." In the 1930s the Gwinns, with their father, had begun acquiring various tracts, ending with a total of 1,921 acres, on which they had established a flourishing cattle-grazing and tobacco operation. Thanks to their strong sense of stewardship, the surrounding farmlands were in far better shape than the village itself.

In any case, the cost of a true restoration would be enormous, and the level of organization such a task demanded seemed beyond reach. Even a warning note sounded in March 1956, when fire gutted one of the original stone buildings, could not hasten action. So was the "wonderful village" simply doomed to perish through decay, accompanied perhaps by further commercialization? It certainly seemed that way. Saving it, everybody agreed, would be a tall order, and it would call for finding the answers to a number of questions. How would such a project repay the time and effort it would require? Should the buildings be preserved for their own sake, or was it the ideas and culture of the builders that would make the restoration of Pleasant Hill worth all the effort it would demand? Or should such a project have higher aspirations?

First: Who were the Shakers and what did they have to do with the people of Central Kentucky?

CHAPTER II

The Vision of Mother Ann

❧

One afternoon in 1957, as a young minister named Don Graham sat gazing out of the window of a Greyhound bus bound from Lexington to Harrodsburg, he became aware that the driver was beginning to address the passengers. Using a microphone as if he were a tour guide enlightening his flock, the driver declared: "Ladies and gentlemen, we will be going through a little village where the men and women really knew how to get along. You will notice that there will be two doors on these buildings. The men lived on one side and the women lived on the other." That was the burden of his little speech.

If people then or at any other time knew nothing else about the Shakers, they knew that the members of this sect had strange and perhaps even incomprehensible ideas about the relationships that ought to prevail between men and women. These ideas traced directly back to one of the more remarkable women in history, Ann Lee, who was born in 1736 into a blacksmith's family in the English Midlands. To most people at the time, Ann would have seemed just another working-class girl destined for an obscure existence of fourteen-hours-a-day drudgery. She never spent a single day in school but like thousands of other children of the slums was put out to work in the Manchester cotton mills.

In two important respects, however, young Ann Lee differed markedly from most of her working sisters: She had a great deal of determination and drive, and at an early age she developed some very unusual ideas about sex.

She believed that biblical prophets were sending her spiritual messages telling her that it was sinful for a husband and wife to have sexual relations and that, consequently, though she was only a child, she must not stand idly by at home but must make every effort to argue her mother out of engaging in such impure activities with her father—who seems to have expressed strong and angry disagreement with her point of view.

Though Ann's outlook changed enough as she grew up to allow her to marry one Abraham Stanley (his name had various spellings), in 1762, she appears never to have felt at ease in this situation; then came a series of tragedies. Ann gave birth to four children, three of whom died in infancy; the other child was sickly, too, and lived only a few years. Such, she knew in her heart, was the awful result of her yielding to the depraved side of her nature. But she still had a husband, and he still had conventional ideas about marital relations. What should she do now?

As it happened, Ann had access to spiritual guidance from persons who saw the world very much as she saw it. A few years earlier, in 1758, in pursuit of escape from the debased and sinful reality amid which she lived, she had joined a small and earnest sect whose animated worship services had earned it the derisive nickname "Shaking Quakers" (just as the members of a later sect would become "Holy Rollers"), although its handful of members included disaffected Anglicans and dissenters, or Methodists, as well as Quakers. The head of the sect suggested a simple solution to Ann's problem: she should practice sexual abstinence. Ann accepted this counsel, but, accustomed to acting energetically in all situations, she found herself unable even to abstain from something in a passive manner. Instead, she engaged in days of great agonizing and lamentation on the state of the world until she emerged, as it would have been put two centuries later, "born again." Then came the transcendent experience, her life's moment of crystallization. In 1770, after being thrown into prison for disrupting an Anglican church service, she experienced not only a vision but a high-level revelation: She herself was nothing less than the fulfillment of the second coming of Christ; Jesus had appeared to her and told her so. His great promise to the world, made more than seventeen hundred years earlier, had now been fulfilled.

When Ann emerged from jail and told her fellow Shaking Quakers about her revelation and her consequent decision to redeem mankind from the consequences of sin, they did not, as one might imagine offhand, respond with skepticism or disapproval. The eighteenth century was indeed a time of schisms, sects, and new denominations (notably the Methodists, who date from just about the year of Ann Lee's birth), and, besides, it was a credulous age. (So, for that matter, was the late twentieth century, an era in which, for example, an American cult leader could persuade his followers to swallow lethal doses of poison in order to prepare themselves for a ride on a spaceship.) Since the Shaking Quakers already were looking for Christ to return at any time, Ann's refinement of their established expectation seemed likely enough, and this determined and dynamic woman, though illiterate, seemed a perfectly appropriate vessel for the revelation. The couple who had established the Shaking Quakers not only accepted Ann's vision but willingly took the logical step of hailing her as their leader and passing on to her the title of Mother; henceforth, she would be known as Mother Ann Lee (her family name actually was Lees; she deleted the *s*).

Mother Ann's vision now became translated into a new religion, the United Society of Believers in Christ's Second Appearing. It rested on the foundation of celibacy, defined as a pure state and an absolute essential for the attainment of spiritual distinction. God was both male and female; Jesus represented the male principle, and the female principle was manifested in Mother Ann; or, as it was also said, Christ was the spiritual Son of God, and Mother Ann was the Spiritual Daughter. (One point that has never been completely clear is whether the Shakers believed Mother Ann to be the actual female reincarnation of Christ or a prophet foretelling a second coming in female form.)

The Shaker worship that grew up could hardly have differed more from Anglican forms, with its singing and dancing, shaking and shouting, and speaking in tongues. Mother Ann soon declared that she had seen in a vision that "God has chosen people in America," and, indeed, what better place could the Shakers find not simply for the free practice of their religion but for the establishment of the heaven on earth—the utopia—they sought than this great and rich continent with endless room for newcomers and new ideas? In May 1774, with eight followers, Mother Ann boarded an old tub of a ship called the *Mariah* at Liverpool for the voyage across the

Atlantic. (Somewhat surprisingly, one of the travelers professing his adherence to the principles of the faith and his devotion to the leadership of Mother Ann was the long-bemused Abraham Stanley.) Thus, during the summer that saw the English colonists in America moving toward the establishment of their own new commonwealth by setting up the first Continental Congress, this tiny band of English utopians was crossing the sea bearing its own dream of an American Eden.

The utopian dream almost came to a sudden end. When the *Mariah*—barely seaworthy, and certainly not suitable for a transatlantic voyage—encountered a storm, a wave ripped one of the rotted timbers loose, and water poured in through the gap in the hull. Though the ship appeared to be in imminent danger of foundering, Mother Ann showed no fear but devoted her efforts to soothing the worried captain. "Be of good cheer," she is supposed to have said with her habitual great assurance, "there shall not a hair of our heads perish. We shall all arrive safe in America. I just now saw two bright angels of God standing by the mast, through whom I received this promise." And in the next moment these angels made good on their promise: unlikely as it seemed, a huge wave lifted up the loose timber and slapped it neatly back into place, and, thanks to this miracle, the *Mariah* and her passengers did indeed survive the crossing.

During their first weeks and months in America, Mother Ann and her followers had to struggle simply to survive, but within two years they had established a permanent settlement at Watervliet, New York, outside Albany. By this time Abraham Stanley, having experienced some second thoughts about the soundness of Mother Ann's sexual doctrines, was urging her to relent and live like everybody else. Not surprisingly, she turned him down categorically. "However pure her motives," commented a journalist writing about the Shakers a hundred years later, her husband "thought himself badly treated, and consoled himself by pursuing a course diametrically opposite to the one she had adopted." By turning to other women, Abraham became perhaps the first Shaker apostate.

Just ten years after landing in New York, Mother Ann succumbed to the accumulated stresses of her extraordinary life, to poverty, imprisonment, and the continuing demands of charismatic leadership. Dying in September 1784 at the age of forty-eight, she left behind an amazing achievement—a flourishing New World movement that, led by strong successors, would soon include ten communities, Watervliet and New Lebanon (which became the Mother Colony) in New York and eight in New England. And within a few more years the word would spread westward and southward.

A t the beginning of the nineteenth century, newspaper readers in the Northeast began seeing reports of a great religious revival out on the frontier, in Kentucky. By this time the state had more than two hundred thousand people, who lived in widely scattered settlements but had been coming together in vast camp meetings, with hundreds of wagons gathering on hilltops. As a later writer told the story: "Thousands of people sang, cried, danced, whirled, fell into trances, barked like dogs, spoke in tongues, proclaimed visions, and were saved."

Among these northeastern newspaper readers was Mother Lucy Wright at the Shakers' Mother Colony at New Lebanon. News of such a dramatic and promising religious upheaval proved irresistible, particularly in view of one of Mother Ann's visions: "The next opening of the gospel will be in the southwest; it will be a great distance, and there will be a great work of God." On New Year's Day, 1805, three Shaker brethren—John Meachan, Issachar Bates, and Benjamin Seth Youngs—set out from New Lebanon for the exciting new mission field in the West. Traveling on foot, with their bags strapped on a single horse, they went down to New York City and on through Philadelphia and Washington to Virginia and then Tennessee, and up through Cumberland Gap into Kentucky. The missionaries arrived at Paint Lick, in Garrard County, on March 3, and just four days later, at the settlement's Presbyterian church, they gave the "first Public testimony of the gospel in the western Country."

What quickly drew the attention of the three Shaker missionaries were the camp meetings over in Bourbon County, with the preaching of Barton W. Stone, the Presbyterian pastor at Cane Ridge who had presided over the great revival of August 1801 and would go on to found the Christian Church (Disciples of Christ). But these visitors do not appear to have been greatly impressed by Stone, who respected them but disagreed absolutely with their view of marriage, and after a stay of only two days they went off to Warren County, Ohio (northeast of Cincinnati), where they "found the first rest for the soles of [their] feet having traveled 1,233 miles in two months and twenty-two days." They also found a landowner named Malcolm Worley, who, within five days of their arrival, became the missionaries' first convert in the West. Others—actually, an entire congregation—quickly joined as well, leading to the establishment of Union Village, near Lebanon, Ohio, which would become the Shakers' chief center in the West.

After their successful mission to Ohio, the three men came back to Central Kentucky. Here, in August 1805, occurred the central event for the future of the Shakers in Kentucky: Benjamin Youngs and two of the Ohio converts met three men from Mercer County—Henry Banta, Samuel Banta, and Elisha Thomas—who "were determined to hear [them] speak" and "drew them to a private house for the purpose." After experiencing the flow of Benjamin Youngs's eloquence, the listeners "opened their minds" to Shakerism, with Elisha thereby becoming the first convert in the area. Thomas soon dedicated his 140-acre farm on Shawnee Run, a broad creek, as the site of a Shaker community.

By early 1806 Elisha had been joined in his conversion by members of many local families, the roll including, in addition to the Bantas and Thomases, such names as Shields, Vibbard, Maxwell, Sasseen, and Dean. As many as a thousand people came to services in barns, listening to preaching and engaging in singing and dancing through the night. Believers from Mercer and nearby areas began moving to Shawnee Run, and on December 3, 1806, forty-four members entered into a covenant, written with the guidance of the elders at Union Village, "dedicating themselves and all their property to the material benefit of each other," and thereby accepting, as well, the other cardinal Shaker tenets—open confession of all sin; celibacy; and separation from the world.

This action represented the formal beginning of the Shaker colony in Mercer County, the first in Kentucky. A year later one of the missionaries reported to Mother Lucy, back in New York, that this flourishing new village was located in a "thick settled place of Kentucky," a state that "contains a great deal of very beautiful land." Knowing the appeal of level topography to the practical-minded farming Shakers, he added, "There is no mountain in sight and the soil is rich and fertile."

CHAPTER III

On God's Time

❀

Within a few years of coming to Shawnee Run, the Shakers had bought or received as donations some three thousand acres of meadowlands in the area, and by 1812 they had moved their village up the slope, about a mile and a half away, to the spot that gave the colony its permanent name—Pleasant Hill. The Shawnee Run location, with its water supply, remained the Shakers' industrial area, with a sawmill, a gristmill, and a linseed oil mill. The Bluegrass farmland, as Thomas D. Clark noted in his account of the Pleasant Hill Shakers, "was of top quality and it was almost impossible for an industrious people to fail economically on it." And the Shakers, as devoted and disciplined a community as could be imagined, had no thought whatever of failing.

By 1823 the village had 439 inhabitants—it grew not only by conversion of adults but also through taking in homeless children—and, as the Shakers acquired more and more land for fields and orchards, their holdings soon reached forty-five hundred acres. All this farming represented true pioneering, calling for willing hands and untiring backs, since the land had never been cultivated and had to be grubbed—cleared of stumps and roots—before crops could be planted. But a report drawn up in 1833 could state: "We have between 2,000 and 3,000 acres of wheat, rye and oats. Besides our flax and 100 acres of Indian corn, broom corn and potatoes." The orchards were extensive, too, with as many as eight hundred fruit trees yielding apples, peaches, pears, cherries, plums, and quinces.

The Shakers based their society on communal living. Men and women lived in the same building and mixed in groups, but they never acted socially as couples. The Believers at Pleasant Hill were organized into three communal groups, called families, each of which usually had about fifty men and fifty women. A family would function as a semi-independent social and economic unit, with its own "dwelling house"—in which the members would cook, eat, sleep, and hold family worship—and its own barns, shops, fields, and herds. The sexes did not mingle at meals or at work, and they entered and left their dwellings by separate doors, but this separation carried no implication that either was superior or inferior to the other. Perhaps not surprisingly, since the sect had been founded and led by a woman, the Shakers practiced true equality of the sexes, with women and men having the same authority; the economic activities of each family were directed by two deacons and two deaconesses. A Shaker family was considered "brothers and sisters in the Lord."

In 1812, the Shakers of Pleasant Hill began the work that would form their great material legacy, not only to their area of Kentucky but to the entire nation and the world. The families with all their activities were going to require not only dwelling houses but an administration building, a school, a church, a post office, and various workshops and other specialized buildings. All this work of design and construction would be accomplished over a period of years, but not in any haphazard or improvised fashion. Instead, the village of Pleasant Hill would come into being according to a definite plan drawn up by one of the most remarkable of the Shakers, a young man of twenty-three named Micajah Burnett.

Young as he was, Burnett quickly proved himself mature in judgment and skilled in administration. Like other notable builders, he made no small plans, and he produced buildings unrivaled in Kentucky in their time. His first dwelling house, for the East Family, set the pattern, standing three stories high, topped by a towering attic, and measuring fifty-five by forty-five feet. It sat on a limestone foundation that enclosed a deep basement; the walls were brick, with limestone trim. Everything that went into the construction of this building—stone, brick, lumber—came from Shaker property and was cut, formed, shaped, and trimmed by Shaker craftsmen and laborers. Construction, supervised by Burnett and carried out by the labor force at hand, with no special equipment, proceeded with remarkable speed. Begun in 1817, the building was ready for use within two years. Next came the similarly large-scale West Family House, completed in 1822. For reasons not under Burnett's control, including internal Shaker politics, the Centre Family House took longer, not being completed until 1834.

Along with the dwelling houses, Burnett planned and supervised the construction of a most essential building, the Meeting House, which, clapboard rather than brick or stone, seemed modest alongside the imposing family houses. However, it presented the designer with a special challenge. Because of the vigorous physical action involved in Shaker worship services—they believed that they could literally shake themselves free of sin, as God was supposed someday to "shake the heavens and the earth"—the great hall had to be unobstructed by pillars or stanchions to spare enthusiastic celebrants any painful collisions, and the walls and supports needed exceptional strength to enable them to withstand the shock waves sent out by all the shaking. A Pleasant Hill visitor from Virginia who attended a service in an earlier building later wrote that after a period of relatively orderly dancing, the worshipers increased the violence of their actions and "by one impulse they now broke order in which they stood and each column whirled within its own limits, in vertical commotion, throwing their heads, hands, and legs in wild disorder, occasionally leaping up and uttering a horrid yell." Then "shrieks and yells followed in alternate succession till by their violence and incessant fury of their dancing, the worshippers were exhausted. Some sank to the floor, whilst others were scarce able to get to their seats." Engaging in this sort of activity in a room with posts and pillars obviously could be hazardous to the Shakers' health, and hence the ingenious Micajah Burnett created an array of interlocking cantilevered trusses to support the roof and ceiling; the notching and fitting were carried out with remarkable precision.

Through the years, Burnett produced a variety of other buildings needed to keep Pleasant Hill functioning, but one of them, begun in 1839, became perhaps the best known of all and contains the most celebrated architectural feature of the entire village. Described by one writer as "the most exuberant of all Shaker buildings," the Trustees' Office, or administration building, differs from the earlier buildings in its reflection of Greek Revival style rather than the Federal style that originally influenced Burnett. The upper two floors of this building were reserved as rooms for a special and vitally important group of Shakers, the "traders" who carried the products of the village to "the World" and, thus being worldly, dwelled apart from their fellow Believers. These floors are reached by twin spiral staircases, so subtly cantilevered that they seem to float upward without support. The staircases, both sturdy and delicate—with treads of blue ash, risers of golden poplar, and banisters of cherry—represent what Thomas Clark called Burnett's "almost intoxicated spasm of romance."

The Shaker traders became important surprisingly early in the life of Pleasant Hill. Already, in 1816, the community had moved beyond production for subsistence to the creation of a variety of goods for export to the world. To reach that world with their goods, the Shakers created a road from the village along the palisades to a spot some 450 feet above the river, and down below they put up piers and warehouses. They built flatboats at the landing, and these soon were carrying brooms, shoes, barrels, tanned skins, woolen goods, fruit preserves, and cheeses from Pleasant Hill via the Kentucky and Ohio rivers to Louisville, and from there the Shaker products made their way down the Mississippi to New Orleans, setting a pattern for trading with the Deep South that would form a basic part of the village economy until the coming of the Civil War.

The Shakers' dedication to constructive innovation led them to experiment with cross-breeding livestock, an activity that involved them in a partnership with Kentucky's most illustrious political figure, Henry Clay; the partners even imported a bull, the famous Orizimbo, from England. The Shakers went on to establish one of America's largest herds of registered Durham Shorthorn cattle, and they also introduced fine sheep to the area. (But they would have nothing to do with mules, looking on these hybrid animals as examples of perversions of the natural order of creation.)

As time went on during the second quarter of the nineteenth century, the villagers of Pleasant Hill produced an array of products prodigious in both variety and volume. A good year would yield them 8,000 bushels of corn, 3,600 bushels of oats, 3,500 bushels of wheat, 2,750 bushels of rye, 400 bushels of Irish potatoes, 2,000 bushels of sweet potatoes, a half ton of cheese, 800 pounds of honey, and 3,400 pounds of wool. They not only marketed the fruit from their abundant orchards but operated a nursery business, selling apple, peach, and other fruit trees to the people in neighboring towns. (Some of them made frequent trips to Lexington to consult on fruit tree grafting with one of the town's pioneer horticulturists and nurserymen, Hector Hillenmeyer.)

Like their brothers and sisters from the other colonies, the Shakers of Pleasant Hill became widely known for the brooms they made. Whether, as is often said, Shakers at one colony or another actually invented the flat broom remains an open question, but no one anywhere engaged in debate about the quality or the popularity of Shaker brooms. In the year 1850 alone, Pleasant Hill turned its fields of broom corn into nineteen thousand finished products, all of which were sold.

Shakers developed the selling of seeds in packets, or envelopes, and on a national, not a local, scale. Similarly, though they were not the first to produce herbal medicines, they turned this activity into another business that flourished on a national scale. In a typical mid-century year they would market twenty-five hundred to three thousand pounds of herbs, shipping the bulk down the river but also keeping Central Kentucky apothecaries stocked.

On top of all this, the Shakers set a good table, with plenty of beef, mutton, chicken (but, after 1841, no pork), a great variety of vegetables, and "buttered waffles, fritters, doughnuts, baked dumplings, peach pies, apple pies, pieplant [rhubarb] pies, puddings, sweet cakes." A visiting correspondent for a Cincinnati newspaper gave his readers a rapturous report, summing it up with "more glorious cookery, I have never met with."

Within a span of years not much longer than a single generation (if these celibate people could be viewed in such a conventional way), the Shakers had become known everywhere not merely for hard work but for ingenuity and originality, for devotion to efficiency and to excellence in design and product. The circular or buzz saw, for instance, was said to have been developed by a Shaker woman after she watched two men laboring with a crosscut saw. Other Shakers had the idea of attaching a vacuum pump to a tank to make possible the concentration of milk or other liquids; this vacuum pan led ultimately, by way of evaporated milk, to a distinctively twentieth-century phenomenon, Elsie the Borden Cow.

Of all the Shaker products, it was the furniture that won the most lasting popularity, with its clean and simple lines that made it seem much more akin to the styles of a century later than to those of its own time. Describing a 1971 show of Shaker creations, Susan Keig, a Chicago designer, commented that she saw "the spare lines of Shaker objects as eminently contemporary and adaptable for continuing use." The Shakers, she thought, were "unconscious in design. They had an intuitive sense of design."

But excellence marked the work of the Shakers not simply in design but in everything they did. A Kentucky state senator declared in an 1837 speech on the floor of the Senate: "Let a stranger visit your country and enquire . . . for your best specimens of agriculture, mechanics and architecture, and, sir, he is directed to visit the Society of Shakers at Pleasant Hill." What lay behind this remarkable achievement? Did Shaker missionaries conduct talent searches, seeking potential converts on the basis of IQ or artistic talent or executive skill and then enticing them into renouncing the world and joining one of the communities? Certainly many Shakers in the beginning days and through the years displayed a great range of talents, but the Believers' overall efficiency and excellence may have been due not so much to the possession of special abilities as to their devotion to a central and simple spiritual idea. They believed that they occupied their place on earth in order to do God's work—as it was said, by putting their hands to work they gave their hearts to God—but they further believed that they must eliminate anything that interfered with the use of their time and abilities in God's service. They thought, in other words, that they must "save God's time." The "pins," or pegs, on their peg boards encircling the walls of each room served, for instance, as clothing hooks or as places to hang chairs when a room was being cleaned or when an open floor was needed; if the Shakers could have known the word "multipurpose," they would have loved it. All the variety of Shaker household and farming gadgets served the same aim of efficiency. If embellishment helped a device work better, that was fine, but decoration for its own sake would merely waste God's time. Thus both the clean lines of rooms and furniture and all the clever devices for kitchen and farm represented the material manifestation of a spiritual idea.

"Both simplicity and unity, in the Shaker experience, are very affirmative," observed Virginia Weis, a student of the Shakers. "To see Shaker furniture—and life—just as 'stripped of ornament' and somehow barren of all human pleasure, is to fail to see the whole point of Shaker simplicity. To be truly simple is to know one's self honestly, yielding neither to pride nor to false humility."

The Shakers hold a special place in American history as the first communitarians, or collectivist group, organized in the New World. Though the number of Shakers never rose above perhaps forty-two hundred, the visible worldly success of these otherworldly utopians also played an important part in world history—it helped convince Friedrich Engels, coauthor of *The Communist Manifesto,* that he and Karl Marx were onto something sound with their idea of communism. One of Engels's articles contains this illuminating sentence about the Shakers: "Among these people there are none who have to work against their will and none who search for work in vain." Speaking specifically of the people at Pleasant Hill, Engels declared that "they are rich, free and happy." There was "no discord," said this dedicated utopian; "on the contrary, friendship and love rule throughout their abode, and in all parts of the same there is order and regularity the likes of which do not exist."

Certainly these observations held much truth, although Engels had never actually seen Pleasant Hill and obviously was peering across the Atlantic through a veil of wishful thinking. The Shakers had indeed achieved a remarkable degree of prosperity, they did not practice austerity for its own sake but—unlike the members of many other sects and cults—found a great deal of enjoyment in life, and they treated people outside their community with great goodwill. They turned nobody away, a policy that led to their extending hospitality to "Winter Shakers," tramps and drifters who sought out the colonies when the leaves began falling from the trees. A writer studying "communistic societies" in the 1870s even decided that "men are not naturally idle" because these people who came to the Shakers at the beginning of winter "with empty stomachs and empty trunks, and [went] off with both full as soon as the roses [began] to bloom"—even these poor would "succumb to the systematic and orderly rules of the place, and do their share of work without shirking, until the mild spring sun tempts them to a freer life."

Yet, like any other utopia, this Shaker Eden had its serpents. The unnatural nature of the sexual arrangements produced continual tensions and a consequent and unremitting looking-and-listening vigilance by the leaders of the community to try to ensure that no pairing-off took place. From platforms atop the dwelling houses, observers surveyed the village scene, following the members as they went about their daily routines. Even during religious services, elders watched the dancers through two small windows looking down on the floor to make sure no irregularities took place. (These observers also kept an eye on any visitors to make sure they engaged in no misbehavior, either.) But a Pleasant Hill journal keeper noted in December 1883: "Marion and Henry Scarball who have been living in the C[enter] F[amily] some years past got Denica Perkins & Sally Monday in a Family way between them this summer. This is the kind of Shakers we have now days." When an elder asked the young men to leave, they refused to go unless they received cash, Henry asking fifty dollars and Marion seventy. The diarist declared: "This is awful." Of course, neither Shaker vigilantes nor any other guardians of sexual virtue could ever rationally hope to achieve complete success in their efforts at surveillance.

Desertion from the society constituted a continuing problem, sometimes with a man and a woman going off together. Women who "went to the World" often departed with the intention of marrying a man who was not of the Shaker faith. As one chronicler noted, "stories have come down of the love affairs of the Believers, who, although bound by their faith to life-long celibacy, could not, in many instances, withstand the impulse of youth or overcome the urge of later years." As time went on, more and more members left the community in order to get married, a trend that played an important part in the ultimate dissolution of the order.

The departures of decamping men and women did not go unjudged by the keepers of the Pleasant Hill journals, large leather-bound books in which every kind of item from national news to notations on the stages of the river was recorded in meticulous copperplate script. For comment on "absconders," the diarists drew on a neat repertoire of disapproving phrases. When Ann Edwards "went to the World" from the Centre Family, a diarist

noted: "How foolish and unwise in this great day! What sorrow and an-
guish awaits thee, poor deluded soul!" After Lydia and Mary Secrest also
left the Centre Family, another journal keeper shook his head sadly: "Silly
lambs you will wish you were in the fold when the wolves get you!" Another "silly lamb" was Tabitha Shuter, who "left the East House for the
wide, cold and heartless world."

One joint departure several years earlier, however, had seemed to speak
for itself: "William Taylor went from the East House before daybreak and
Catherine Shuter from the same place in the evening." (Catherine, perhaps, was not quite as innocent a lamb as Tabitha.) But when John Jacob
Howri absconded from the East House, he was written down as "a wild
chap." At that, he fared better than the decamping Paul Jacobs, who received this good-riddance comment: "A great annoyance and pest to the
Society." Scribes, in fact, did not usually write with charitable pens. The
absconder would be called a "worthless scamp," or the departure would be
summed up in such phrases as "a puff of trash has blown away," "dead
limbs will drop off," or "so the Devil has got you at last, you good-for-
nothing."

Perhaps the most spectacular interaction between the village and the
world, however, was the case of Caroline Whittymore, the "Harlot of
Harrodsburg," as the diarist of the day characterized her. She and her brother
James had come to Pleasant Hill as orphan children, but after she matured,
the elders, appalled at her "wicked ways," drove her out of the community.
Unfazed, Carolyn soon returned, accompanied by "one or two of her associated prostitutes under the influence of liquor." Rebuffed in her request to
see James, she ignored the orders of the elders, sought her brother out, and
took him away at the point of a horse pistol. (James saved his soul, however, by returning a few days later.)

Harriet Martineau, one of the most widely read of the many nineteenth-century English journalists and writers who crossed the ocean to
take the measure of the United States and share their conclusions with the
public back home, found the Shakers excellent economists but ignorant
and superstitious moralists. "I have never witnessed more visible absurdity
than in the way of life of the Shakers," she declared. "Their spiritual pride,
their insane vanity, their intellectual torpor, their mental grossness, are

melancholy to witness." Getting to the point, she then observed: "Their thoughts are full of the one subject of celibacy: with what effect may be easily imagined. Their religious exercises are disgustingly full of it. It cannot be otherwise," she said, "for they have no other interesting subject of thought beyond their daily routine of business. . . . Their life is all dull work and no play." Granting the Shakers' "entire success, as far as wealth is concerned," the writer drew a conclusion marked by towering condescension. If such wealth, she asked, was "the result of co-operation and community of property among an ignorant, conceited, inert society like this, what might not the same principles of association achieve among a more intelligent set of people, stimulated by education, and exhilarated by the enjoyment of all the blessings which Providence has placed within the reach of man?"

On August 1, 1861, the keeper of the day's Pleasant Hill journal recorded an event that put the utopian community squarely in the world: "A company of soldiers called home guards passed through this village to-day and mustered in the street."

Pleasant Hill and all the other Shaker colonies already faced continuing serious problems. Though they had flourished wonderfully during the first half of the nineteenth century, they found America changing around them, as the rapidly developing new industrial world began offering the kinds of attractions and inducements that agrarian communities could not match. As some of the able-bodied men began leaving for the cities and the number of conversions shrank, the elders put greater stress on recruiting orphans, but the net figures nevertheless showed an ominous decline. From another point of view, the Shakers, with their ingenious but small-scale production of goods, found themselves in a losing race with the new technology that was making possible the rise of the industrial state.

Now, in 1861, the whole country was "greatly agitated on the question of negro slavery," with "the North and South being arrayed against each other." The Shakers of Pleasant Hill found themselves squarely in the middle—geographically, as residents living literally in the center of a border state, and politically, as holders of a can't-win position. Northern loyalists expected them to support, and even fight for, the Union—after all, they claimed to be abolitionists, didn't they? In the highly charged atmosphere in this divided state, these Union supporters could find no sympathy for the pacifism that formed one of the fundamental Shaker beliefs. As for Confederate sympathizers, they expected no support from the Pleasant Hill abolitionists. The Shakers themselves found their moral and economic interests in collision: their beliefs committed them to the Union, but the South had long formed their great trading hinterland. This by no means meant, however, that they wavered in their sympathy for the North and abolition. But it dramatized what a calamity war would be for the community, especially if Kentucky itself should become a battleground.

The state guard assembling on the village street on that August day in 1861 symbolized the trouble in itself. These young men were not Union supporters but were preparing to march south to join the Confederate army. The Shaker journal keeper saw this as "the most singular and sad spectacle ever witnessed since creation," with the people of the United States throwing away "the best government ever vouchsafed by heaven to mortals on earth" and preparing to butcher and murder each other for no reason "except disappointed ambitions, rivalry and jealousy." Some behavior for "true Christians[!]"—and a much more thoughtful and even eloquent commentary for the journal than the ritual and perhaps obligatory observations always made about absconding apostates.

In August 1862, with the Confederate invasion of Central Kentucky, some of the Shakers' worst fears began to come true. During the following months, Union and Confederate troops swept back and forth through the area: the fast-moving Rebel raiders of Colonel John Hunt Morgan, the famous "Thunderbolt of the Confederacy," and the thousands and thousands of troops involved in the Battle of Perryville, the largest engagement fought in Kentucky. October 11, 1862, wrote the journal keeper, was such a day as had "never been witnessed on Pleasant Hill before, and God grant that it never come again!" In the aftermath of the great battle, the soldiers demanded food—"Our feeding them rose from 300 to 1,000 per day and night with thousands of others begging for a small bit to eat"—and, sometimes even more urgently, demanded horses. The Shakers supplied as much food as they could, to anyone who needed it, at no charge even when pay was offered, but they took great care to hide the best horses and, as far as possible, made only the older animals available to their uninvited guests. The generosity of the Shakers so impressed Colonel Morgan that he refused to allow two of his men to "press" a pair of horses.

Though other actions came in 1863 and 1864, the worst was over for Pleasant Hill, but the end of the war in the spring of 1865 brought no happy return to prewar days. Like all of Kentucky, if to a lesser degree, the Shaker community had suffered disruptions and rifts that left the old consensus severely damaged, with insubordination frequently taking the place of the old obedience to the elders and eldresses. All across the country, spiritual ideas that had seemed compelling to many fifty and even twenty-five years earlier found no roots in the new economic order, which was about to begin the colossal expansion that would produce the industrial American giant of 1900; even the fine Shaker jams would lose out to fruit preserves produced on a mass scale. People everywhere looked now to real cities, not to dream utopias.

Although Pleasant Hill had its moments during the remainder of the nineteenth century, the period essentially saw faltering leadership and dwindling membership, with few conversions. Even the "glorious cookery" that years earlier had delighted the Cincinnati reporter did not survive the slow decline; in January 1888 a diarist who obviously remembered better days recorded this sour comment on the cuisine: "We had the awfulest Supper we ever saw tonight, Bread, butter, Pie, milk, Tea, Coffee & Molases. Now beat that if you can."

A few years earlier, in 1882, a little-known incident had delivered a heavy financial blow to the community. In a classic case of deception and fraud, a con man from Waynesboro, Ohio, had gulled the guileless Shakers into signing notes that tied up some of the land and led to an 1896 judgment against them in federal court for the impossible sum of $30,000. This disaster had led to the sacrifice of the Meeting House, the Trustees' House, and several hundred acres of farmland.

Finally, in 1910, the twelve remaining members acknowledged that the community had come to the end of its life as a religious order. These survivors deeded the eighteen hundred acres that now remained of the Shaker lands to George Bohon, a Harrodsburg buggy manufacturer, who agreed in exchange to look after the Believers as long as any of them remained alive; however, Bohon died in 1916, while the last Shaker survivor, Sister Mary Settles, lived on until 1923. Now free of their obligations to the Believers, Bohon's heirs moved quickly to sell the land, the buildings, and the Shaker possessions that remained with the property; the once-thriving community now had many owners and no longer an essence.

The most striking part of the century-long Pleasant Hill story was not the fading away of the community but its earlier rise to the kind of success that attracted the attention of far-off Friedrich Engels and even won the reluctant respect of Harriet Martineau—an economic success that brought with it the spread of much kindness and goodness. The Shakers were no doubt strange and peculiar, as their neighbors tended to say, and they certainly would not get very far if they should try again in the twenty-first century, but they many times proved themselves humanitarians devoted to good works and worthy stewards of the land they claimed. All in all, the Shaker movement constituted a remarkable memorial to one unlettered, charismatic woman who planted a uniquely personal vision across an ocean. And, as great builders, the Shakers turned much of that vision into lasting brick and stone.

CHAPTER IV

The Past—Preserved, Restored, Remade?

❧

On April 11, 1799, one day before his twenty-second birthday, a promising young Kentucky lawyer named Henry Clay was married to Lucretia Hart, the daughter of Colonel Thomas Hart, a well-to-do pioneer Lexington merchant. The wedding took place at the home of the bride's family, a substantial two-story brick house of some twelve rooms, which sat at the southwest corner of Second and Mill streets in the young city.

After Colonel Hart's death several years later, his son, Thomas Jr., sold the house to John Bradford, who in 1787, with his brother, Fielding, had established the *Kentucky Gazette,* the first newspaper to be published west of the Alleghenies. In 1789 John Bradford had also published Thomas Johnson's *Kentucky Miscellany,* the first book of a literary nature to come from a Kentucky press. One of the founders of the Lexington Public Library, in 1795, this early-day leading citizen published a number of other notable works in his long career, including a book that later became extremely rare and a coveted item among bibliophiles, *Narrative of the Life and Travels of John Robert Shaw, the Well-Digger.* Bradford lived in the house until his death in 1830.

Sitting diagonally across Second Street from Gratz Park, the "Bradford house," as it was often called, belonged to what became Lexington's most fashionable neighborhood. In 1848, the house served as the setting for a second wedding of special interest, when a young man who, like Henry Clay, would also rise to national prominence, John Hunt Morgan, was married to Rebecca Gratz Bruce. Still later, Mary Jane Warfield Clay, divorced wife of the combative emancipationist Cassius Marcellus Clay, moved into the Bradford house, accompanied by her daughter Laura, a controversial figure in her own right as one of the leading voices in the national women's rights movement.

By the 1950s the house was possibly the oldest, as well as one of the most storied, of the eighteenth-century houses still standing in Lexington. And then, one day in March 1955, it was gone.

No one in the 1950s could summon much surprise at the sight of a property owner demolishing a 1792 house to make way for a parking lot. That was what governments were doing, too, and on a much larger scale, leveling whole neighborhoods and districts for slum clearance or, as it had come to be more euphemistically called, urban renewal. But this time, the destruction of this single house did not pass unnoticed by all Lexingtonians. Concerned residents of the Gratz Park neighborhood, in particular, suddenly wondered what might happen to the house directly across Second Street from the Bradford house. Once the finest of all the elegant residences on Gratz Park, but now divided into apartments and up for sale, this house had been built in 1814 for John Wesley Hunt, possibly the first Kentuckian who could be considered a genuine tycoon, with his extensive mercantile (including the making and marketing of hemp products), banking, and horse-breeding interests; his wife was Francis Scott Key's cousin. The home's graceful spiraling staircase led many to attribute the design of Hopemont, as the house was called, to the noted architect Benjamin Latrobe.

Later, Hunt's grandson and namesake, the ubiquitous John Hunt Morgan, had occupied this house, and still later his great-grandson Thomas Hunt Morgan, the eminent geneticist who won the Nobel Prize for Medicine in 1933, had lived there. Something must be done; the house must be saved—otherwise, one day soon, the town might wake up to discover that its past had simply vanished, turned into parking lots. That was the feeling.

Perhaps there was something new in the air in 1955, in Lexington and in other cities. Just that same year, after seeing the venerable City Market demolished to make way for a parking garage, citizens of Savannah were organizing to stop the razing of a handsome 1821 brick structure, the Isaiah Davenport house. It was not that the developers saw no value in the old house. Quite to the contrary: they planned, after disassembling the building, to sell the bricks while they were proceeding to convert the site into still another parking lot. The people of Savannah had already acquired a good deal of experience in battling traffic experts, road builders, and other interests that sought, sometimes successfully, to dig up and demolish the city's famous and distinctive old squares in order to replace them with boulevards. Now, responding to what one preservationist later called "blatant destruction of a part of the fabric of the city," community leaders went about establishing a private, nonprofit corporation, the Historic Savannah Foundation, with the first aim of saving the Davenport house.

Could Lexington undertake the same kind of preservation?

E ven the term "historic preservation" did not enjoy wide use in the 1950s; no full-length book on the subject had yet been published in the United States. As for preservation itself, carried out for whatever purposes—ideological, aesthetic, archaeological, commercial—it had followed a tortuous, up-and-down course in American history. There was never anything automatic about it; people often seemed to believe that for Americans the past and its symbols should hold little importance and only the future counted.

As far back as 1816, concerned citizens in Philadelphia had been forced to organize to keep the state government from tearing down Independence Hall and selling this valuable downtown property to developers. Before the city government intervened to buy the building from the state, two wings of the building were gone and the woodwork had been stripped from the room in which John Hancock and his fellow rebels signed the Declaration of Independence. The familiar tower that has long identified the building dates from 1828, not from the Revolutionary era, and thus provides an example of historic restoration (not preservation, because nothing remained of the original tower; having deteriorated badly, it had been removed almost thirty years earlier).

In 1853, to block a group of businessmen who wanted to buy Mount Vernon and turn it into a hotel with great water views, the governor of Virginia asked the heir living in the house, John Augustine Washington Jr., the president's great-grandnephew, to sell the property to the state. Since Washington lacked the money to maintain the buildings and grounds himself, he strongly favored this proposal, but he tagged the estate with a hefty price—$200,000 in 1850s dollars. Not putting such a high value even on this symbol of patriotism, the state legislature and the federal government both refused to fund the project. A South Carolina woman who had seen Mount Vernon from the deck of a riverboat wrote to her daughter that she was "painfully distressed at the ruin and desolation of the home of Washington." She continued, "Why was it that the women of his country did not try to keep it in repair if the men could not do it? It seems such a blot on our country." Very well, said the daughter, Ann Pamela Cunningham, who responded to this brief but pioneering preservationist manifesto by organizing the Mount Vernon Ladies' Association, which took up the cause. Within only five years, after conducting a national campaign, the group had raised the needed money and had managed to come to terms with the somewhat contentious Washington; the ladies and their successors have owned Mount Vernon ever since. Late in her life Ann Cunningham made her own addition to the slowly developing preservationist creed: Washington's home should remain as close to his time as possible, she declared, saying, "Let one spot in this grand country of ours be spared from change." The successful effort to save Mount Vernon established a trend that has proved permanently true of preservation efforts—the assumption of leadership roles by women. It also seemed to say that preservation is an activity in which private citizens, not government, should take the lead.

Unfortunately for those who hoped that George Washington's legacy could serve as a national rallying point amid the tremors of approaching civil war, this success at Mount Vernon came too late. Even so, by saving this private house for public purposes the association had created a precedent or model, though one fated often to be ignored for more than a century. (It is also worth noting that among the casualties of the Civil War was John Hancock's birthplace in Braintree, Massachusetts, which, as land values rose, found no group to save it from developers. Another war casualty was John Washington himself, who died in combat fighting for the Confederacy.)

In the ensuing decades, groups sprang up across the country on the Mount Vernon Ladies' Association model, buying and restoring houses that had been occupied by leading patriots. Michael Wallace, a self-styled radical historian, sourly observed that "these projects enabled the elite to associate themselves and their class with the virtuous and glorious dead." These efforts also had the effect of bestowing permanent popularity on eighteenth-century architecture; Professor Wallace saw this as promotion of a "class aesthetic" favoring buildings "hallowed by association with the entire pre-immigrant social order." In 1900, looking at the point from a slightly different angle, a Mount Vernon officer had considered the involvement of children with historic sites and characters a help in "the making of good citizens of these many foreign youths." Either view—either emphasis, perhaps—makes it clear that preservationists during the second half of the nineteenth century acted primarily from ideological and social motives rather than out of aesthetic concerns. But architecture slowly began to take its place as a second consideration, so that a building might be considered worthy of being preserved even if nobody famous had ever lived in it.

In addition to individual houses, another piece of the past engaged the attention of certain prominent preservationists—the Early American village, whether artificially assembled or resurrected in place. These projects, far too large to be carried off or even conceived by the usual citizen groups, were the work of millionaires and billionaires. The two greatest of these, which offer an instructive contrast, both came out of the 1920s.

Henry Ford brought together buildings from across the country—stores, an inn, a courthouse, a windmill, Thomas Edison's laboratory, and various others—for his personal monument to nostalgia, Greenfield Village, outside of Detroit. "Greenfield Village," observed one writer, "where Ford . . . embalmed American life as it was before the Model T." The car mogul himself considered the village an "animated textbook" to be used for teaching like any other schoolbook. Ford's creation represented a sort of pre–Disney World, except that the buildings were real, not copies, even though they had been brought from their original locations to Michigan. Preservationists have since classified Greenfield Village as an "outdoor museum," though they professionally deplore the moving of buildings from their original sites.

In Virginia, John D. Rockefeller Jr. created what continues to be the most famous of such town museums—as familiar to us, one writer said, as Niagara Falls or the Washington Monument—when he waved his golden wand over the sleepy and shabby pre-Revolutionary capital of Virginia to create Colonial Williamsburg. In the mid-1920s a mixture of buildings from four centuries stretched along both sides of the town's business artery, Duke of Gloucester Street, many of them in one or another stage of dilapidation. A decade or so earlier, the *Richmond Times-Dispatch* had enjoyed a good laugh at Williamsburg's expense when the city council refused to appropriate any money to have the municipal clock wound. Calling the town a "Lotus land," the newspaper said that the "Lotusburgers" had found a simple way to solve all their problems by stopping the clock. Nevertheless, Williamsburg, when the Rockefeller project began, was a lived-in, functioning town, with gas stations, laundries, and other modern (if unappealing) buildings mixed in with the survivors from earlier centuries.

In the astounding new project, workers demolished more than 700 buildings that had been built after the eighteenth century, restored 83 survivors of that century, and reconstructed 430 others of which nothing remained, putting up most of them on their original foundations. Rockefeller arranged for the Chesapeake & Ohio Railroad to take its distracting twentieth-century operations out of town, and his workmen went even further, uprooting the local Confederate (hence, inescapably, nineteenth-century) monument from its natural place on the Palace Green and carrying it off to an obscure side street, to the vocal distress of the United Daughters of the Confederacy, already deeply disturbed over the force and scope of this new Yankee invasion. The Williamsburg corporation also made sure of its aesthetic security by buying up some 3,000 acres of land to create a buffer zone around the 130-acre core.

All of these actions took place within the framework devised by the project's teams of architects, archaeologists, and historians, who had the mission of leading the way back to the eighteenth century. Overall, said Rockefeller, he had sought "an opportunity to restore a complete area and free it entirely from alien or inharmonious surroundings." In 1931 a twenty-five-year-old native of Midway, Kentucky, James Cogar, fresh from studies at Yale, took up a task for which little precedent existed—he was given the remarkable opportunity to become the first curator of Colonial Williamsburg, then just three years away from its opening in 1934. "They had no notion of what a curator was," he said, "and I had less. We learned it together."

Cogar proved to be a notably good learner, and his reputation grew with the acclaim Williamsburg received and the popularity it won. Mastering his trade as he went, he paved the way along an untrod path so well that he began setting national standards in historic eighteenth-century interiors, demanding perfection, always striving to render a building or a room as it had originally been. At one point during his curatorship, he had responsibility at Williamsburg for the hostesses, the craft shops, the costume shop, and flower arranging in addition to the collections. When he resigned his position in 1948, Cogar had earned recognition as one of the country's leading experts in eighteenth-century furniture and furnishings. As an official publication of Colonial Williamsburg summed up his work, his "dedication, taste, and perception resulted in contributions that were invaluable."

American Heritage would title a 1960 article on Williamsburg "The Town That Stopped the Clock"; in fact, the town had done much more than that. It had parsimoniously stopped time back in 1913, and in the late 1920s and early 1930s had gone much further, turning the clock back for perhaps a century and a half, creating a remarkable time bubble that would become the showplace of twentieth-century preservation. Although generally admiring the results of these gargantuan labors, the author of the *American Heritage* article, a *New York Times* correspondent who was himself a native of Williamsburg, had one caveat, expressing some perturbation at the "aseptic implausibility of so much fresh paint and polished brass and tidy lawns and prim table settings." Professor Wallace dismissed Colonial Williamsburg as a town with no dirt and no smell. How could that be called history?

After the establishment of the British National Trust in 1895, representatives had crossed the Atlantic to see whether they might help the Americans set up a similar organization for preserving historic buildings, but the visitors soon concluded that their hopes were premature. In the ensuing years, specific groups like the Mount Vernon Ladies' Association and the Thomas Jefferson Memorial Foundation ably served their individual purposes, and the National Park Service oversaw such properties as Independence Hall and the Franklin D. Roosevelt home at Hyde Park. In addition, regional groups such as the Society for the Preservation of New England Antiquities flourished, and several cities—Charleston, South Carolina, the pioneer, and New Orleans and Annapolis—had adopted ordinances mandating preservation. But not until half a century after the British preservationist missionaries had come and gone had the picture in the United States changed enough for Americans to begin discussing the need to create a broadly based national, private organization, an adaptation of the British National Trust, that could knit together the work of widely scattered preservationists, take title to historic properties, and mobilize citizens in defense of the past.

The first phase came in April 1947 with the establishment of the National Council for Historic Sites and Buildings, under the leadership of Ronald F. Lee of the National Park Service, the agency that in many ways acted as the godfather of the movement; David E. Finley, a Washington figure whose importance was only partially suggested by his position as director of the National Gallery of Art; and George McAneny of New York, president of the American Scenic and Historic Preservation Society, which, despite its sweeping name, had been founded for the specific purpose of saving row houses on Washington Square in Manhattan. This new council gave itself the assignment of establishing an American national trust, and it acquired its first staff member in August 1948 when the National Park Service provided Frederick L. Rath Jr., a young historian from Dartmouth and Harvard then working at the recently opened FDR home site, on loan as executive secretary.

As it happened, Betty Walsh, a recent graduate in history from the University of Kentucky, had just come to Washington with the aim going to work for the National Park Service as a historian. She also had thoughts about going overseas in an army job, but "that was when the Berlin airlift was starting," she said, and "my mother had other ideas." At the Park Service she encountered Fred Rath, who offered her a job: "He was looking for a secretary to set up a new organization called the National Trust for Historic Preservation." Amused at the memory, Betty Walsh said, "I always told Fred that he hired me because I knew half as much as he did, and he didn't know very much. He didn't want a smart-alec type of Washington secretary." But in the lively Betty Walsh he certainly had not acquired a restrained and submissive associate, either.

Working from an office on an upper floor of the building that housed Ford's Theatre, one of America's most historic sites, this new team, with the support of board members of the national council, worked on developing a budget, gathering support from foundations, and preparing a proposed bill to submit to Congress for a charter for the proposed trust. The bill won the strong endorsement of the *New York Times,* which declared in one of its four supporting editorials that "these are days when, more than ever before, we need the inspiration of the past as we advance into a troubled future." The measure moved briskly through the House of Representatives and, passed by the Senate after some procedural delay, was signed by President Harry Truman on October 26, 1949.

The temporary hold-up in the Senate certainly had nothing to do with money, since the preservationists had not sought federal financial support and the bill explicitly ruled it out. This charter by Congress blessed the National Trust for Historic Preservation with status as a quasi-governmental entity and thus gave high-level recognition to the dawning of a new day in the United States for preservation. Presumably the National Trust could proceed to raise its own money through attracting private support, just as the National Gallery of Art had attracted collections worth tens of millions of dollars and had raised sustaining dollars as well. The preservationists in Washington were to find, however—as a group of preservation-minded Kentuckians would discover not many years later—that the story would not be so simple: art and preservation were different philanthropic animals, with different kinds of appeal and different dynamics. More important in the long run, however, historic preservation had now arrived on the national scene.

But preservation would not have this scene to itself. In the 1930s, a New Deal program inaugurated by Secretary of the Interior Harold Ickes, had found useful work for more than a thousand unemployed architects in surveying and recording in photographs and detailed drawings all the "historic" buildings in the country—more than six thousand of them. In the late 1940s and through the 1950s and well into the 1960s, however, a powerful countercurrent would obliterate much of the national legacy that engaged the attention of preservationists and local historians—including, by 1966, the destruction of more than half the buildings that appeared in the 1930s surveys. Twin streams fed this countercurrent—slum clearance and highway construction. As one historian put it, "Developers rammed roads through cities, demolishing whole areas; urban renewal then devastated much of the remaining landscape." To another commentator, "Clean-the-slate urban planning sought to erase the burden of the past." In the mid-1950s, this slash-and-burn approach to reviving cities gained great impetus from the passage of a federal highway act under which a gasoline tax would provide the funding for the creation of the Interstate Highway System. An urban historian declared: "Though transportation had been the most powerful force throughout American history in shaping the development of cities and concentrating greater proportions of the population in urban areas, vast sums of money were now going to be spent on a highway program related neither to a national urban policy nor a comprehensive transportation program."

Thus in the mid-1950s the federal government looked benignly on the slowly developing movement to preserve historic, culturally valued, or simply well-loved places and buildings from the American past. But the actual federal dollars were going elsewhere, funding forces and agencies that, in the name of building, were dismantling much of the material manifestation of that past. The new citizen preservationists, it appeared, would have to look elsewhere to fund their dreams.

CHAPTER V

Nickels, Dimes, and Options

꽃

Te Lexington citizen probably most disturbed by the destruction
of the Bradford house and the threatened loss of Hopemont lived
not in the downtown Gratz Park neighborhood but several miles
away, on the northern fringe of the city. That made no difference—Joseph
C. Graves, vice president and operating head of the old-line family clothing firm Graves, Cox and Company, seemed to look on all of Lexington as
his neighborhood, and the well-being of your neighborhood was something you worried about. A short, slender man of forty-nine, Joe Graves,
though remarkably public-spirited, lacked the glum seriousness with which
many doers of good tend to view the world. Widely popular, he enjoyed
jokes and witty exchanges, and he never really outgrew his childhood love
of pranks.

During World War II, Graves had made a unique contribution to morale
by writing letters "to his footloose correspondents"—some thirty or forty
friends in all branches of the service in all parts of the world—telling them
what was going on at home. "They give a marvelous picture of Lexington
during the war years, with a light touch," said Graves's son, Joe Graves Jr.
(Speaking of "the seriousness of the liquor situation," Graves told his correspondents that "an honest bottle of bourbon is as hard to find as a nice girl
in a Limestone Street bar," and he gave regular reports on his comic ven-
detta with a moralizing army vice officer, a hapless Captain Witherspoon,
who kept a nervous eye on the activities of GIs and WACs either stationed

in the area or in transit.) Graves would type his letter on Sunday and take it to the office the next day to be mimeographed and mailed. After returning home following the war, his footloose friends honored him with a dinner of appreciation.

Graves read widely and had a number of aesthetic interests; in particular, he devoted a great deal of time to printing, a hobby he shared with his wife, Lucy. Under the tutelage of Victor Hammer, the Viennese artist and typographer whom he had been instrumental in bringing to Transylvania College (as the school was then known), the Graveses established the Gravesend Press in the basement of their house, where they set type by hand and printed and bound books. The first Gravesend offering, *The Mint Julep*, a Christmas keepsake published in 1949, made quite a splash and was reprinted a number of times; other Gravesend books drew such patrons as the British Museum, the Houghton Library at Harvard, and the Newberry Library in Chicago. At several different times Graves also taught graphic arts at Transylvania College, and since 1953 he had been president of the Henry Clay Memorial Foundation, the organization that preserved Clay's residence, Ashland, as a public museum.

Even before the demolition of the Bradford house, Graves had dreamed of making some kind of organized effort to preserve Lexington's landmarks from the wave of postwar destruction assaulting every city in the country. The leveling of the house at Second and Mill streets, almost overnight, and the threat to its neighbor across the way then pulled the trigger. Moving rapidly, Joe and Lucy Graves rounded up a group of concerned friends, including Carolyn Reading (soon to become the wife of Victor Hammer), Lucretia Johnson, Van Deren Coke, Suzanne Hamilton, Edward W. Rannells, and a number of others. As noted earlier, through the hundred years since Ann Pamela Cunningham founded the organization that saved Mount Vernon, women had taken prominent roles in projects to save American material history, and preservationist activities in the Blue Grass in the 1950s and 1960s would conform to this same pattern; in an era in which well-to-do women were generally not involved in the job market, philanthropic activities depended heavily on their knowledge and energy. (The style of the time is shown by their listing in documents and news stories by the names of their husbands; thus "Mrs. Lawrence Brewer" rather than "Juliette Brewer.") Michael Wallace, the historian who objected to preservation-by-elite, perhaps had not reflected that without the labors of such elites, the coming of preservation would have been delayed by more than a century and might never have happened at all. Who else had the time, the money, and the inclination?

The organization founded by Joe Graves and his friends, called the Foundation for the Preservation of Historic Lexington and Fayette County, held its first organizational meeting on April 19, 1955, with Graves, Sydney Combs, Van Deren Coke, and Carolyn Reading being named as the organizing committee. This group devised a structure of functional committees and put together a slate of officers who would serve for the first year; the minutes of one session tell us that "great informality and much enthusiasm marked all meetings during this time." The organization received its papers of incorporation on July 18, but, not waiting for this formality, the members of the foundation had already assessed themselves for $2,666 to make the down payment on Hopemont, which the owner, Mrs. Carey Gratz Johnstone Thomas, had agreed to sell for $37,334; the foundation borrowed the remainder at 6 percent interest over fifteen years. Thus the local preservation movement had gotten under way.

Though they had gone into action to save a particular building, just as the preservationists in Savannah were doing, the members of the Lexington group apparently were acting independently, not yet aware of the parallel between their efforts and those in Georgia. As volunteers involved in a very concrete project, they found themselves called on to produce "sweat equity" as well as cash. After hard years as an apartment building, Hopemont—which after some discussion received the designation the "Hunt-Morgan House"—needed work inside and out, starting with an overall cleaning and the removal of features added through the years, such as a first-floor bathroom. The group decided to hire professional painters to do the outside of the house, but the preservationists themselves wielded the brushes on the inside walls and trim.

A crew of volunteers cleaned up the yard and began laying brick walks, and furnishings came in from various donors, enough to give a period feel to the interior of the house. This effort to reclaim the house may have had its technical faults and deficiencies, but, on the other hand, these were pioneer preservationists. In any case, the foundation leaders deemed the house ready to be opened to the public in October, just six months after the birth of the organization.

The foundation had as its purpose, Joe Graves told the government in his application for a federal tax exemption, the "preservation of buildings, structures and personality which have historical significance in Fayette County, Kentucky." For some time, however, the Hunt-Morgan House itself continued to form the center of activity. Aside from dues, membership assessments, and donations, the only income came from entrance fees to the house and the sale of souvenirs, cards, and gifts, and the rent payments from the two remaining apartments in the house.

Although the foundation acquired a thousand members in less than a year, money came in with lamentable slowness. In February 1956, to bolster the treasury, the executive committee authorized the president to buy a thousand "Norwegian glass ashtrays" at 54 cents for sale at $1.00, but such operations produced no revolutionary results. In June 1957, for instance, the house took in $493 from all sources and spent $343, leaving a balance of $150; the foundation's general account held a balance of $818. Not surprisingly, Suzanne Hamilton, the recording secretary, noted that "the assessment letter will be sent out to the membership soon." The money on hand would go for such items as the purchase of additional brick, for $25, to complete a walkway and the acquisition of dirt for the herb garden. At this meeting Graves presented some bad news indeed: termites and dry rot had almost destroyed the two floors in the back wing of the house. Repairs, if the executive committee adopted the recommended plan, would cost $492.35; the committee accepted the plan. Somebody else pointed out that the gutters needed repairing and that "certain plumbing improvements were imperative."

Along with these uninspiring particulars, however, the committee had something far more exciting to discuss. At the suggestion of Clay Lancaster, an architectural historian from Lexington who then lived in Brooklyn Heights, New York, Joe and Lucy Graves had become involved with the National Trust for Historic Preservation, and in little more than two weeks, preservation at the highest level would be moving into Lexington, when the Foundation for the Preservation of Historic Lexington and Fayette

County played host to an event called the Blue Grass Preservation Short Course, in cosponsorship with the National Trust; financial support was coming from the Lilly Endowment of Indianapolis, which had already contributed to the preservation of the Hunt-Morgan House. This would be only the third such short course anywhere, the National Trust having held one at Cooperstown, New York, in 1955, with an encore at the same site in 1956. The local foundation had the benefit of some expert help in designing the arrangements for the conference—Betty Walsh, who had continued to work for the National Trust through the Truman years, had gotten married in Washington, and she and her husband, Robert Morris, had now moved to Lexington. Serving as registrar and general factotum, Mrs. Morris reported that, as of the day of the committee meeting, sixty-seven persons had made reservations for the conference.

During the three days of the short course, those attending received a full load of instruction. Designed as a study of the unique architectural and historical heritage of the Blue Grass region, the program presented a variety of notables—architects, historians, musicologists, experts on early furniture and furnishings, and specialists in the operation of historic houses—who conducted panel sessions, gave illustrated lectures, and held private consultations with participants. The list of those appearing included Richard Howland, president of the National Trust, former fine-arts chairman at Johns Hopkins; James L. Cogar, of Colonial Williamsburg fame; Barbara Snow, managing editor of *Antiques* magazine; Earl H. Reed, preservation officer of the American Institute of Architects; Clay Lancaster; and numerous others. As a special feature of the program, Lancaster led a field trip to some of the old houses and gardens of the area. The tour included lunch at the inn at Shakertown, at which F. Gerald Ham, a young University of Kentucky doctoral candidate with detailed knowledge of the history of Pleasant Hill, gave a talk on old Shakertown. This excursion put Shakertown in a prominent place in a number of preservationist minds. Indeed, it was, James Cogar later recalled, "the first exciting moment in which people felt something might be done about the restoration of the village."

At the next executive committee meeting, in September, Graves and his associates could bask in the praise the conference had received from persons at the National Trust, and at the Lilly Endowment as well. Altogether, the speakers seemed to have stirred up a good bit of general interest in the preservation of historic sites, including Shakertown; this great response made it obvious that "the foundation must get into larger fields of preservation this coming year." Activity was already moving ahead in relation to one field. Robert Houlihan, a Lexington lawyer, had completed his work in gathering material for the foundation to present to the Planning · and Zoning Commission for the preservation of Gratz Park. This step would soon lead to the establishment of the first Historic District in the Commonwealth of Kentucky.

The meeting brought another, and perhaps more portentous, piece of news from Graves, involving Barry Bingham, editor and publisher of the *Courier-Journal* of Louisville. As Kentucky's leading liberal philanthropist, Bingham was often the first person sought out by anybody in the state whose cause needed start-up money or an infusion of cash to keep it going. Wealthy and worldly, the Binghams (Barry and his wife, Mary, were often spoken of this way) not only could offer financial support to a project but had unlimited connections, across the commonwealth and internationally; they also initiated numerous activities of their own in various fields, from ecology to music. The *Courier-Journal* prided itself on circulating in all of the commonwealth's 120 counties, from the mountains to the Mississippi, and one editor observed years later, "There was an old saying that the two most influential institutions in Kentucky were the University of Kentucky College of Agriculture and the *Courier-Journal*," because each was established in every county in the state. In politics Barry Bingham was said to be such a kingmaker that he had dictated the makeup of the 1959 Democratic state ticket, with Bert Combs running for governor and Wilson Wyatt for lieutenant governor.

Graves reported to his associates that this uniquely potent state leader had talked with him about the desirability of preserving Shakertown, a long-cherished dream of Graves's. (Joe Graves Jr. recalled a day, sometime in the 1950s, when, as he sat in the back seat while he and his parents were driving through the village, his father declared, "These buildings all need to be preserved. It's very important to do it." Looking around at these empty buildings, Joe Jr. thought, with a young person's customary disdain

for parental ideas, "That's the most far-fetched thing I've ever heard. But
he really meant it.")

Presumably encouraged by his talk with Bingham to take further action, Graves and a representative of the Lilly Endowment then met with
Burwell Marshall, the Louisville lawyer who owned important buildings in
the center of the village. A jaunty character who, rather daringly for those
days, sported a navy blue beret, Marshall offered to sell these holdings for
$100,000, but cagily asked that "no publicity be given this decision as it
would not be received well by the other property holders." At this point,
the project had been floated only as a matter of general interest; no plan
existed for financing it. Possibly the National Park Service could operate
the village, some thought, or a state organization might do the job with the
help of grants from the Lilly Endowment. A few weeks later, after a visit
from Marshall—who said that he had bought a number of Shaker artifacts
to give to the purchaser of the land—Graves, together with Sydney Combs,
planned to meet with Bingham in Louisville to talk more about the project,
but at this point everybody was still optimistically looking to the state government to carry much of the financial load.

In early October the foundation renamed itself the Blue Grass Trust
for Historic Preservation, thus allying itself fully with the National Trust.
But despite its increasing scope and ambitious aspirations, the organization's
finances remained mired at the nickel-and-dime level. The Hunt-Morgan
account had picked up $20, for instance, from the sale of cocktail napkins
made by Mrs. Sterling Coke, and the kitchen clock had been disposed of
for another $10; an arcane transaction involving the re-covering of a couch
had netted a $35 refund for the house treasury.

O thers besides the group in Lexington had Shakertown on their minds.
For Harrodsburg—the oldest permanent settlement in Kentucky,
located just seven miles farther along Highway 68 past Pleasant Hill—the
restoration of the village would constitute a great local project with a kind
of importance beyond its meaning for Lexington or Louisville. Jane Bird
Hutton, the proprietor and editor of the *Harrodsburg Herald,* the local
weekly, had one simple creed: "Shakertown must be saved." In her news
and editorial columns she waged a continuing campaign for the restoration

of the village and lent encouragement to anybody or any group that seemed likely to take effective action on such a project.

An imposing and "very sharp" woman, as one acquaintance described her, Miss Hutton was positive in print as well as in person and had a good many allies among local leaders. Although she saw Shakertown as an important part of the American heritage and believed that its preservation would "add culture and atmosphere to the county," she strongly advocated the project for economic reasons, seeing it as a "sleeping giant" that every year would draw thousands of tourists and thousands of dollars to Mercer County; it could mean as much financially, she believed, as a factory that employed six hundred to eight hundred people. (Miss Hutton had long and sincerely supported on its merits the idea of restoring Shakertown, but such involvement has not always been necessary for projects of this kind to win local support. In Seneca Falls, New York, for instance, local merchants strongly supported the establishment of a Women's Rights National Historical Park—even though, according to a village trustee, they didn't "give a hoot" about the town's importance in the history of feminism—because of the business this attraction would bring in. "I mean," the trustee said, "if you've got Old Faithful in your town, you're in favor of geysers.")

During the two years following his first meeting with Barry Bingham, Joe Graves had continued to talk with various persons in Louisville concerning Shakertown. Looking for likely possibilities, this ad hoc group had thoughts of involving Berea College in the project. No informed person can have supposed that this particular institution would contribute any cash to the endeavor, but Bingham, a Berea trustee, had suggested that the college's famous woodcraft operation reproduce and sell Shaker furniture; action was, however, slow to follow.

In May 1959 Graves and Bingham came to Harrodsburg to meet with Burt Rowland, president of the chamber of commerce, and Minnie Ball Goddard, of the historical society, to talk about plans for Shakertown. Thus came together the representatives of the two cities whose interest in Shakertown was primarily historical and aesthetic with persons whose county might almost be transformed by a renaissance at Pleasant Hill.

Just a few weeks later, on June 16, Harrodsburg celebrated its 185th birthday with a dinner at the Shakertown Inn, sponsored by the local historical society, which had as its theme the idea of restoring the village as a historic shrine; members of the county chamber of commerce joined in the discussion of this plan that "would bring . . . tourist dollars into the county." At the dinner, two chamber of commerce representatives reported that they had discussed the project with five owners of Pleasant Hill property, and at a subsequent meeting the representatives put a precise figure on the table: the property owners wanted a total of $362,000. Burwell Marshall was now asking $90,000 for his village property on the north side of the highway, and Bob and Bettye Renfrew wanted $75,000 for the inn. Obviously these were impossible figures for a project that didn't even have a bank account, but the group chose a committee—made up of several Harrodsburg leaders together with Graves and Bingham, who were present—to meet with Marshall for some possibly more realistic discussion.

Despite these profound fiscal problems, the Harrodsburg leaders capped the June 16 dinner by cheerfully announcing the formation of a committee to explore methods to restore some fifteen buildings at Pleasant Hill and make the place a historical and tourist site. Members said they hoped to restore the broom factory, carpenter shop, preserve-making plant, and tannery. The committee included Mrs. Goddard, chair; Colonel George M. Chinn, secretary of the Kentucky Historical Society, a colorful gentleman who in the 1930s had served as a bodyguard for Governor Happy Chandler and had won renown as the world's leading expert on the machine gun; W. H. Phillips, Harrodsburg city attorney; and Edwin Freeman, a local real estate broker. (Looking ahead later, Mrs. Goddard said that if any progress should be made toward restoring Shakertown, the group would try to win state legislation that would prevent shoddy buildings and other undesirable elements from springing up in the vicinity. No county historic area or any other kind of zoning existed.)

Though they were keenly interested in the project, these Mercer Countians showed no signs of regarding Shakertown as their own turf and looking on the Lexingtonians as interlopers. As Vivian Landrum, a young woman in the group, recalled, everybody knew what a great challenge the project represented; whoever carried it out would need all the help that could be found. Many of the Harrodsburg group, along with persons from Bourbon and Woodford counties, became members of the Blue Grass Trust.

Robert Jewell, a horseman whose farm lay on Highway 68 near Wilmore and thus not far from Shakertown, became an important link between the counties. "Shakertown has always been big in our family," he said, "to me and to my father before me." Very much a man about town who knew everybody and also knew what everybody was up to, Bob Jewell liked to entertain and was fond of saying that his house made a good bathroom stop for people going between Lexington and Pleasant Hill, since the village didn't offer much in the way of facilities.

As he continued all his negotiations, Joe Graves reported to the Blue Grass Trust board of directors about the "many difficulties involved" in the project; the interested group had not yet "arrived at a sensible and practical plan for running it." He also noted that a close friend, Raymond McLain, president of the American University of Cairo and former president of Transylvania, was expected in Lexington for a visit. Through the years McLain and Graves had talked about the exciting possibilities of a renewed Shakertown, and Graves planned to seek his current advice concerning the project.

If Shakertown ever did get up and running, it seemed that it would have in Graves a leader with the talent to keep it in the public eye. Back in the Depression, as the young advertising manager of Graves Cox, he had made probably his biggest splash when he had created a series of newspaper ads that attracted national attention. Designed to fit a skimpy 1930s advertising budget, the ads featured a line drawing just one column wide. In those days cartoons involving cannibals were a staple of the *New Yorker* and other smart magazines, and cannibal jokes were common. In one ad Graves made use of this popularity, showing two perplexed cannibals staring into a bubbling cauldron from which a third had just escaped. One of the pair asked in wonderment: "Where's George?" The caption then told us: "George is at Graves Cox buying a Kuppenheimer suit." The ads appeared twice a week, each time with a different scene from which George had just made a miraculous getaway. Soon customers began calling the store to suggest new situations from which George might escape; a St. Louis corporation then bought the rights to the concept for national distribution. Later Graves lodged a characteristic complaint with his sister, the mother of twins: "If she had named those boys Graves and Cox, as I suggested, the advertising budget of the store could be reduced fifty percent."

Though McLain would later have considerable involvement in planning for Pleasant Hill, Joe Graves was destined never to have the chance to use his promotional talents on behalf of the village. On June 3, 1960, his colleagues at the Blue Grass Trust, along with many other Lexingtonians, were stunned to hear of his death the night before of a heart attack; he was just fifty-four. "He was a practical joker, and very, very funny," Carolyn Hammer said, remembering him years later, "but he was wise."

Joe Graves's untimely death "set back" the cause of Shakertown, as one observer wrote. "Everybody was devastated when he died," said Betty Morris, and, having lost their only and genuinely loved president, the members of the Blue Grass Trust took some weeks to rally. Early in August, however, the board came together in a meeting at the Lafayette Hotel in downtown Lexington to "set in motion" again the work of the Trust. The list of those present at this important meeting included Lucy Graves; her sister, Margaret "Retta" Wright, who was active in the Red Cross; Carolyn Hammer; Bob Houlihan; and several newer members: Charles Graves, dean of the College of Architecture at the University of Kentucky (no kin to Joe Graves); Warfield Gratz, a well-known local architect with a quintessentially preservationist surname; Dorothy Miles; Hilary Boone, who operated an insurance agency; and Bob Jewell. In recognition of Joe Graves's enthusiasm for the Shakertown project, the board resolved to continue his work and, in essence, named a committee to replace him. As Betty Morris recalled it, the board members began seeing the preservation of Shakertown as a kind of memorial to Graves. Jewell was to be chairman of the new committee and Juliette Brewer, a Lexingtonian who served for a number of years as chairman of the board of Liberty Hall, a historic house in Frankfort, Kentucky, co-chairman; the board also chose Boone, who once described himself as fond of "living with old things and old houses," to be the new president of the Blue Grass Trust.

Events now moved ahead on two tracks. Jewell and others kept on with the negotiations Graves had conducted with Shakertown property owners, and the members of the committee, taking no small view of their duties, set out to analyze the whole nature and purpose of the project. Acknowledging the magnitude of the task and convinced, at the same time, of the great opportunity it presented, they asked themselves some serious questions: Did the preservation effort offer opportunities that would make a continuing contribution to contemporary life? Could this be a successful venture for all those "who have long sought to unite in this preservation effort"? What could be done to accomplish such an undertaking? Behind their philosophizing, the members were moved by a sense of urgency: if the movement did not get going soon, they felt, some of the buildings would deteriorate past the point of redemption. Interestingly, they took a view of the project far beyond the local horizon. The question of "proper usefulness," they came to believe, was "a compelling one in this crucial period of our national development"; only a contribution to society as a whole could justify the expenditure of time, effort, and money the project would demand.

In making a study of the property with its buildings, the committee turned to Gerald Ham, who had become an associate curator at the West Virginia University Library but had been researching Pleasant Hill and the Shakers with scholarly zeal for some eight years. A slim, intense young man, Ham had no doubts whatever about the importance of the restoration project. "I have spent many an enjoyable hour tramping all over Pleasant Hill and finding the remains of their various industries," he wrote the committee. "Pleasant Hill was the pride of western Shakerism. It was one of the largest societies, and by all odds was the most beautiful of all the western Shaker villages." Then, making a key point, he observed: "More important, it seems to me, it is the only one of the seven western settlements that remains much as it was a hundred years ago." He enclosed a data sheet on the buildings and their histories and functions. In another message he declared that Pleasant Hill was "the most complete Shaker village remaining in the United States." It was "no exaggeration to say that Pleasant Hill represents one of the more significant of the few remaining unspoiled historical sites west of the Appalachians."

The committee also sought the counsel of a variety of nationally prominent preservationists, including Richard Howland, who had now moved to the Smithsonian as head curator of the Department of Civil History, and Helen Bullock, both of whom had come to Kentucky to take part in the 1957 short course . After paying a return visit to Pleasant Hill, they assured the committee "that the preservation of the village would be an invaluable conservation of an important part of our American heritage; would provide a rich source of material on a century of cultural and social history in the Ohio Valley; and that its loss would be a tragedy." Other advisers concurred. Consulted specifically concerning the buildings themselves, Charles E. Peterson, director of the Historic Houses Division of the National Park Service, and Clay Lancaster both pointed out the good fortune represented by the fact that no modern buildings intruded on the rural setting and that the existing structures had not undergone significant alterations.

Assured now—and certainly not against its collective will—of the desirability and feasibility of preservation, the Shakertown committee moved on to its other great concern, the question of what use to make of it. Asked for his thoughts about what should happen at a restored Pleasant Hill, Raymond McLain did not disappoint the group but responded with three long memoranda, giving the group the phrase "proper usefulness." A man of high seriousness who "always knew what to say," as Carolyn Hammer put it, the college president declared that the village must be a living center, not simply a collection of beautiful buildings. The preservation effort itself should seek to "reveal the original beauty, utility, and strength of the structure, and the simplicity and discipline of the life lived by the Shaker Community." With this result achieved, the aim then must be "to utilize the property and facilities in such a manner as to improve the quality of contemporary life. These purposes are complementary, each contributing to the other."

Thus guided, the committee spent a great many hours talking with various persons about specific programs that could contribute toward the goal. The suggestions included establishment of an exhibition center of Shaker life and culture; revival of some of the Shaker industries, such as making preserves, brooms, and cooperage (not only barrels, but small vessels called piggins and noggins) and packaging seeds; creating a residential center for continuing education, patterned after successful centers in England; installing recreational facilities, so that people would "find stimulation, inspiration, and pleasure at Pleasant Hill"; establishing a press, for the publication of seminar papers and monographs, and perhaps also for a revival of the Shaker periodical *The Western Review*, which could be sent to

"Friends of Shakertown" (Lucy Graves had already offered the equipment of the Gravesend Press).

Feeling some urgency because of spreading urbanization even in Mercer County and also because of the need, in some cases, to "stabilize the buildings," as one of the members, Dorothy Clay of Louisville and Bourbon County, put it, the committee decided right away to acquire options on five pieces of property, with different owners, which would include the village itself and some of the surrounding lands. As it turned out, making such a decision was relatively easy; actually making the deals proved to be another matter entirely.

At a September 14, 1960, meeting of the Blue Grass Trust board and the Shakertown committee, R. B. "Red" McClure, a lawyer hired to represent the Blue Grass Trust in dealings with Shakertown property owners, told the group that Burwell Marshall, whose fifty-six acres included about half of the buildings in the village, had agreed to grant an option on the property, which he valued at $90,000.

Of the other landholders, a father-and-son combination—Clarence Kurtz Senior and Junior—owned thirty to forty acres (this vagueness was due to the fact that no survey had ever been made). The father's land included the old cemetery but had no buildings on it; the son's property, however, took in not only the old broom factory but the combination gas station and store; the father was asking $18,000, the son $35,000. The Kurtzes stipulated that they would not grant an option for a period longer than a year.

The Gwinn brothers, who owned most of the surrounding farmland, had about sixty acres in the village area itself. Herbert Gwinn, who spoke for his brother as well as for himself, wanted $150,000 for this particular parcel and would grant an option for only a month. Believing, with good reason, that the demands of operating a two thousand–acre farm had Gwinn ready for retirement, however, McClure told the committee that the landowner might be more interested in the project than he was indicating.

The final property holder held the key to the whole operation, although even here there was a complexity. The Renfrews not only owned but operated the Shakertown Inn—the building that for the Shakers had served as the Trustees' Office—on which Gwinn held a mortgage. Renfrew wanted

$75,000 for the property and, like Gwinn, declared that he would grant an option only for thirty days. The inn presented a colorful scene and served inviting food, as Dick DeCamp's reminiscence showed, but it was clearly no gold mine. Unanimously considering it "the vital 'first' purchase in the Shakertown project," the committee members also agreed that since the Renfrews were not making a financial go of things and should therefore welcome the chance of a cash sale, they might well accept a counteroffer, possibly $40,000 or $50,000. Possession of the inn would give the Shakertown committee an asset that could be improved and, the committee members believed, turned into a moneymaker.

But one problem loomed before the members: these plans were all very well, but the committee had no money. Should they try to form a corporation and sell stock? A bank loan seemed a likelier possibility, and to investigate, Hilary Boone appointed a committee of Juliette Brewer, Retta Wright, Dorothy Clay, Bob Houlihan, and Bob Jewell. This group certainly enjoyed status and connections in the community, but in two weeks they returned with a negative report: Edward Dabney of the Security Trust Company had turned them down flat.

From phone conversations with Herbert Gwinn, Juliette Brewer had concluded that this landowner did indeed have a strong desire to see the Blue Grass Trust take over Shakertown; perhaps he would urge Renfrew to sell his property for a "fair price." At the same time, the committee would try to raise money by asking people to sign $1,000 pledges; this list would be used as security to pry $40,000 out of a bank. In a note to Lucy Graves, Boone wrote: "As you know, we have had a great many meetings and some of them may have appeared to have been useless; however, I do think we are making progress and trust that our efforts will not be in vain."

Meanwhile, the options needed to be extended—which, despite the talk of thirty-day deadlines, they were. They also became more complicated. By February, far from yielding to any squeeze by Gwinn, Renfrew was turning down an offer of $55,000 while agreeing to settle for $65,000, with $100 payable every month to hold the option. In March, a meeting with the Gwinns began frostily when they appeared to have been upset by tactless remarks McClure had made to them. "After some discussion," Boone told Bingham, "it appeared that money would salve their feelings." This deal had become complicated by the Shakertown group's agreement to acquire a nearby farm and swap it for the Gwinn property; executing this option would require a $10,000 deposit up front. For their part, the Gwinns wanted $1,000 cash up front and another $11,000 when the option was exercised.

Looking back years later at this day-to-day period of prices, options, counteroffers, and hopeful talk of fund-raising, one of the newer Shakertown committee members said: "At this point, none of us knew what we were getting into, how much the restoration would cost, and where the money would come from. We were proceeding on faith, hoping to extend the contracts from time to time until we could find the money to buy the Village property." This newer member's name was Earl Wallace.

CHAPTER VI

"The Beginning Year"

❦

On Wednesday evening, August 9, 1961, in a meeting of the Blue Grass Trust at the Hunt-Morgan House, Bob Jewell announced the formation of a nonprofit corporation to preserve, restore, and use the village of Pleasant Hill. The group would acquire the buildings and land and would "maintain the property in such a manner as to reveal the original beauty, utility, and strength of the structures, and the simplicity of the life lived by the Shakers." The group would also, he said—faithfully reporting the McLain-influenced decisions of the Shakertown committee—"utilize the property and facilities in such a manner as to improve the quality of contemporary life." More specifically, it would restore the village so that it represented Shaker life and culture of a century earlier, and it would institute a varied program of cultural, educational, and recreational activities, with seminars, conferences, festivals, and tours. This child of the Blue Grass Trust, now striking out on its own, would be called Shakertown at Pleasant Hill, Inc.; the members of the Shakertown committee became the organizing board of the new corporation. (The double name, combining the familiar designation of the village with the traditional Shaker name for it, was suggested by McLain.) The incorporators were Hilary Boone, Juliette Brewer, Dorothy Clay, Charles Graves, Lucy Graves, Bob Houlihan, Bob Jewell, Harry Tucker, Earl D. Wallace, and Retta Wright.

The plan won enthusiastic endorsements on all sides. Governor Bert Combs, who generally supported educational and cultural activities and sometimes had funds to contribute to them, declared that he had "com-plete and unqualified" enthusiasm for the idea of preserving this "priceless historical entity." The area's newspapers loved it. The *Lexington Herald* said editorially that "no project that has been suggested in recent years could be of greater value to Central Kentucky than the proposal to restore historic Shakertown"; it could be a "tourist attraction that, properly developed, will return millions of dollars to Kentucky in the years ahead." It could even mean that "Kentucky would have a tourist attraction second only to re-stored Williamsburg, Va., one of the nation's outstanding attractions of a bygone era." The *Lexington Leader,* the *Herald's* Republican afternoon sis-ter, though a bit less rhapsodic, endorsed McLain's ideas about the con-structive use of Shakertown as a justification for the expenditure of time and money that would be required to preserve it, and considered the plan an opportunity for Kentucky to acquire "a tremendous asset to the Blue Grass and the whole state, and a place of interest to the entire nation."

Jane Bird Hutton of the *Harrodsburg Herald* of course gave the project complete editorial support, expressing special approval for the aim of re-storing Shakertown as a "living village," which, she said, had some years ago been the thought of a local citizen, the late Colonel James L. Isenberg. Striking her familiar theme of the job opportunities the restoration would offer, she declared: "We have a gold mine in our county. Let us not fail to see that everything is done by us to assure the program."

No one will be surprised to learn that the *Courier-Journal* applauded Governor Combs's complete and unqualified enthusiasm. "To this," the paper said, "we add an amen." The editorial offered specific congratula-tions to Bob Jewell and Hilary Boone, as the leaders of the group of Cen-tral Kentuckians who were proposing the restoration. Few newspaper readers could know what thought and labor and what endless meetings lay behind Bob Jewell's announcement. Few could realize what an act of faith it still represented.

Several months earlier, though poor in both cash and property, the Shakertown committee had decided on another act of faith. To keep things moving in coordination, the members of the group agreed, the de-veloping project must find an executive director. Though anybody who accepted the job would indeed have to be a person of remarkable optimism and faith, the committee at least had front money to offer: the members and a number of close friends had proved their dedication to Shakertown by putting up the needed cash themselves; in the last three months of 1960, five persons had contributed a total of $10,849, headed by $5,000 from Dorothy Clay and $3,000 from Lucy Graves. The committee also proposed to seek "Founding Sponsors" who would underwrite the expenses of the first two years of operation, estimated to total $60,000; this fund, intended as a short-run, maintenance operation, was seen as separate from the long-range capital fund, which would be built up through a proposed five-year development program, with $1 million as the goal. Despite the talk of such big numbers, anybody coming from very far away to take the director's job would have to have at least some gambling instincts or, perhaps, enjoy independent means.

By spring the committee had put lines out to a varied group of candidates, some of them suggested by the director of the National Trust. In late April, Raymond McLain, who served as a sort of roving consultant to Pleasant Hill, discussed the situation at a lunch meeting in New York with a Wall Street financier who had become interested in the Shakertown project. Unlike McLain, the financier had no particular admiration for the Shakers themselves, whom he considered a group of bizarre misfits, but those great buildings and the challenge of saving them constituted another matter.

The two men agreed that it might take considerable time to find a person who could be effective both as a fund-raiser and as executive director—these being the two chief aspects of the job as they saw it at the time. The group should, however, move quickly to choose a president of Pleasant Hill, McLain said, because of "the reluctance of people to give unless they know who is going to be responsible for the planning of the project and its financial soundness." The financier, Earl Wallace, offered an interesting— and, in the light of later events, amusing—reply to this observation: everybody appreciated the need to find a president, he said, but "we are unable to think of anyone acceptable who might take it." One way or the other, however, if Pleasant Hill was to gather support it needed to have on board the people who were going to run the project.

Though now spending his working time in Manhattan, Earl Wallace was a native of Knox County, Kentucky, and at heart a thorough Lexingtonian. Sixty-two years old and moving toward semiretirement, he commuted weekly from Lexington, where his family lived, to New York and the offices of the investment bankers Dillon, Read and Company at 15 William Street in lower Manhattan—the firm he had joined after spending thirty years in the oil business.

Wallace had certainly not gone through life carrying any torch for Shakertown, but during his years at the University of Kentucky, like many another university blade of the time, he had discovered a particular charm of the village. In those days the inn was located in the East Family House and the tearoom "served marvelous food. A wonderful Sunday dinner—I think it cost a dollar. We tried to save our money to take girls there if we could find a car." (But "I had never heard anyone refer to it as Pleasant Hill," Wallace later said, in expressing his agreement with the idea of keeping the popular name for the sake of local identification.)

In March 1961 the Pleasant Hill personnel search had taken a strange turn. When Richard Howland, the former president of the National Trust, had come to the Blue Grass to advise on the feasibility of the restoration, his personality and ideas had exerted a galvanic effect on the committee. The day after Howland left, Barry Bingham, on behalf of the group, wrote him that he had made "converts among those who had really only come along with the program out of friendship for the chief participants, or a sense of public obligation." Now, said Bingham, everybody had become "warmly enthusiastic and eager to move ahead. As to those who were already zealous in the cause, they have been given a greatly increased faith in the practicality of the project, and a renewed determination to make it succeed." So dazzled had the group been that Bingham went on to offer Howland the job of executive director of the Shakertown organization-to-be. Obviously this was a long shot, indeed, in view of Howland's eminence in the field and his new, and presumably secure, position at the Smithsonian. But, said Bingham, the committee could not resist making the offer "in the hope that a near miracle might make it possible for you to agree to do it." (No miracle was in the offing. He was "completely surprised and very touched," Howland said, by this "tribute that was indeed heartwarming."

But even Bingham's elegant blandishments could not lure him away from the Smithsonian.)

Just a few days after this exchange, Bingham found himself on the receiving end of another proposition—or he would have had Hilary Boone decided to mail a certain letter. In this letter Boone told Bingham that, since the time had come to form a separate Shakertown organization, the group "unanimously and deeply" felt that Bingham should become general chairman of the entire project. This proposal formed part of an organizational plan in which Bingham would cast his aura over Louisville, Cincinnati, and Central Kentucky and a vice chairman would serve as the actual executor of the committee's policies. Obviously, operating with such a structure could raise practical questions, but bagging Bingham as the lead lion of the organization would have constituted a notable coup. If the two dreams could have been combined, Bingham, Howland, and the vice chairman, whoever he might have been, would certainly have made up a potent executive team, but it was not to be. So Shakertown did not yet have either a president or an executive director; even so, the project was not fated to suffer from a lack of leadership.

Though Shakertown did not yet have a president, the executive directorship question seemed to have been settled when, in July, the Shakertown committee chose Ralph McCallister, of Chapel Hill, North Carolina, for the post. A distinguished-looking man in his fifties, tall and gray-haired, McCallister was an acquaintance of Raymond McLain's and came to the project from long experience as vice president and director of program and education at Chautauqua, visiting lecturer in the Maxwell School of Citizenship at Syracuse University, and director of the Adult Education Council of Chicago. This background suggested both that McCallister had leadership experience and that he had the kind of knowledge that fitted him to carry out McLain's concerns about program activities at Pleasant Hill.

McCallister, who was to be paid $10,000 a year plus a housing allowance of $200 a month, would be joined on the fledgling Pleasant Hill staff by Betty Morris, whose cousin, Bob Jewell, had urged her to give up her staff position at the Red Cross and help out with Shakertown full-time; she was hired as McCallister's assistant at $250 a month. They would work in two rooms in Hilary Boone's Massachusetts Mutual office at 2200 Young Drive, in the east end of Lexington; Boone gave them a break on the rent, charging $50 a month, about half of the going price, though one room would be shared with the Blue Grass Trust (perhaps, McCallister thought, the Trust might be willing to contribute $12.50 to the rent; either way it was a complex little situation, with Boone as the chairman of the Trust, about-to-be treasurer of Pleasant Hill, and benign landlord). By late July the office had begun functioning.

Though the *Courier-Journal* had singled out Boone and Bob Jewell for its editorial praise, the "temporary chairman" of the incorporating group was Earl Wallace. Not a member of the original committee, Wallace nevertheless had his own interest in historic landmarks, having been the inspirer and donor of the first such plaque in Lexington, at Ashland, Henry Clay's estate; it was put up in 1937, and Wallace had even composed its text. Because he was still working in New York, flying up on Monday morning and back on Friday evening, he had only limited time for activities in Lexington. But a close friend, Harry St. George Tucker, owner of the Taylor Tire Company in Lexington and a member of the Shakertown committee, asked Wallace to accompany him to one of the group's regular meetings, which were held on Saturday mornings.

No sooner had Wallace joined the committee, it seemed, than he was chosen for the top spot. "At one of those meetings, I probably opened my mouth and said too much and they made me chairman," Wallace once said by way of explanation. But his selection had little surprising about it: the principal problem—often, indeed, the only problem—facing the incorporators was money and how to get it, and even though several of them had enjoyed success in businesses of various kinds, Wallace brought with him the luster of Wall Street. He had also held high executive posts, including a vice presidency of Standard Oil of Ohio. When he proved willing to take on the challenge of the so-called temporary chairmanship, that settled it. Bob Jewell later recalled having felt some surprise, however; he had thought that "this man is too smart to take hold of this business." But take hold Wallace did, so thoroughly that from then on, whatever title others might hold, he would be the true CEO.

Three days after the announcement of the new corporation, at a meeting of the incorporators, Wallace began by proposing a resolution recognizing that "the inspiration for this group to undertake to save Shakertown originated with Joseph C. Graves." The resolution as adopted declared that the organization "to secure, improve, preserve and properly use" Pleasant Hill—note all four points—had come into being as a direct result of Graves's influence.

The *Courier-Journal*'s expression of editorial approval represented only the paper's initial response to Jewell's August 9 announcement. On the following Sunday, readers were told, the paper's magazine supplement would carry a major feature on Shakertown—three pages of color pictures, a story by a leading reporter, and a number of aerial photos and other pictures. When the story appeared, it did indeed cover the subject in encyclopedic detail. Obviously long in the preparation, the coverage had benefitted from detailed help given by Burwell Marshall, who had "always been interested in" the restoration of Shakertown, the paper noted, and now hoped to sell his property to the new organization (as the paper did not note). It was also obvious that Barry Bingham's interest in a subject translated into thorough coverage by the *Courier-Journal*'s staff, even if, despite his heavy involvement in the project for the past four years, the boss took care not to appear in the coverage himself.

Observing that it was "high time some organization took action to preserve the stately old Shaker buildings with their double entrances," the reporter, Gerald Griffin, warned that "after withstanding the ravages of time and the elements, some of them are being destroyed by man." He went on to paint a compelling picture of Pleasant Hill's needs, history, and possibilities. The story was timed to appear with a new kind of event: only four days after Jewell's announcement, not wasting a moment, the Pleasant Hill group was hosting a Sunday open house at Shakertown, from three to six in the afternoon. As Betty Morris remembered it, the prime mover in this project was Juliette Brewer, "one of the greatest entrepreneurs since P. T. Barnum." Wife of Lawrence Brewer, a University of Kentucky agriculture professor who also operated a horse-feed business, Mrs. Brewer had led the campaign to preserve Henry Clay's law office in downtown Lexington and had served in other preservation efforts. "The one thing I always said about

Mrs. Brewer," noted Dick DeCamp, who later directed the Blue Grass Trust, "was that if she wanted a table moved, she got on the other end and helped move it. She was like all the ladies—they all wanted their own way. She was strong-willed, but I always admired her." A Mercer County native, Mrs. Brewer wanted no delay in showing off Shakertown, even though the new organization did not own a single square foot of it. Here again, Burwell Marshall cooperated, this time by making the Centre Family House and two other buildings available for the party. Volunteer hostesses would display drugs and medicines, seed boxes, bonnet forms, looms, and kettles from Marshall's collection of Shaker objects.

"Mrs. Brewer came to me," Betty Morris recalled, "and said, 'We're going to have lemonade, and I've brought you these six pitchers.'" That, with several cans of frozen lemonade, seemed adequate-enough preparation for the hundred or so guests expected for a little open house out in the country, until the cars began coming. "The lemonade wound up in Mrs. Kurtz's country store in the freezer," Mrs. Morris said, "because we didn't have a minute to open it." Some two thousand people crowded into the village that Sunday afternoon, and a number of others tried to stop but had to keep going on Highway 68 because they couldn't find places to park.

On the following Sunday, with fifteen members of the Harrodsburg group serving as hostesses for a second open house, Pleasant Hill greeted more than three thousand visitors, who heard talks from the hostesses on the uses of the buildings and the habits of the Shakers. "Visitors are not satisfied with just a look inside the three buildings open for inspection," said Sterling Tapp, who had been chosen as president of the Mercer County committee affiliated with Shakertown at Pleasant Hill, Inc. "Interest is so great they want to roam the grounds and take a look at all the buildings."

"We were overwhelmed," Ralph McCallister said, but local merchants expressed delight at the crowds for the open houses. Robert Renfrew said that the inn enjoyed a tremendous increase in business, and even a restaurant at Brooklyn Bridge on the Kentucky River, several miles away, reported the biggest crowds for a number of years. Such success encouraged Earl Wallace to announce that the open houses would continue through early November.

Not everybody was thrilled with the unrestored state of Shakertown, however. At one of the open houses, young women from a Harrodsburg high school sorority served as hostesses, with each one stationed at each main door or on each floor to greet visitors and open and shut doors. "The buildings were dusty and deserted," one of the members remembered, "with no lighting except what came in through the windows, and one of the main buildings had hay in it." When she went to leave her building, the other girl stationed there refused to remain by herself, and left, too. She found it just too spooky, "particularly in the late afternoon."

On September 1, Mercer Countians came together in a mass meeting to plan a local fund drive, setting themselves a quota of $40,000—a small percentage of the totals that had been discussed for the project but an impressive figure for a small town at a time when cash had only slowly appeared on the Shakertown scene. A representative of the Kentucky Department of Economic Development came to town to explain the value of the proposed project to the economy of Mercer and surrounding counties. Soon a twenty-foot-high thermometer had sprouted on a downtown street, and almost immediately the mercury rose from zero to $1,000 (*$39,000 to go*, observed the *Herald* jauntily), and then it leapt to $5,500. Having firmly committed themselves in every way to the project, the Harrodsburg leaders did not prove shy about asking McCallister for "further details about the expectations from other areas." How serious, for instance, was Fayette County?

Though program and not promotion was his primary interest, McCallister did his part to spread the word by speaking at every kind of club and function—in Harrodsburg, Lexington, Nicholasville, Berea, Versailles—and Friends of Shakertown groups were beginning to meet in several counties; Mrs. Edward Ray headed this effort. Keeping the autumnal events rolling, Shakertown at Pleasant Hill announced the first annual fall festival for October 5–8, featuring "Kentucky Treasures," some of them Shaker pieces, others from Blue Grass collections—antiques, silver (including the service from the old battleship *Kentucky*), and china. On the meadow between the Centre and East Family Houses a country fair would present prizewinners from the state fair in Louisville. There would also be a flower show and a display of old guns (from Kentucky flintlocks to a Japanese matchlock) from a prominent private collection, and members of Homemakers clubs from three counties would bring canned products and hand-made goods. The food for consumption on the spot sounded much more tempting than the 1888 Shaker fare: country ham sandwiches, homemade cake, and coffee. Mrs. Brewer would preside over the entire event as "general chairman." Some of these features obviously had much less to do with the Shakers than others had, but all of them together served to focus attention on the project and its setting.

Governor Combs opened the festival by lifting a cord of flowers resembling a Hawaiian lei from the two doors—men's and women's—of the Centre Family House. Declaring that there was "no more interesting or romantic spot in the country" than Shakertown, the governor said that the restoration would help make Kentucky the country's leading state for tourists. From then until the end of the four days, Jane Hutton roamed the grounds with her ears open for adjectives used by the visitors in talking about the experience: she noted *unique, interesting, successful, amazing, terrific, fascinating, enjoyable, educational, entertaining, colossal.* It all proved, she said, the existence of a great genuine interest in the Shakertown committee and its attempts to preserve and restore the Shaker community.

Mercer County managed to display its own interest in tangible form: by mid-October the temperature in the downtown thermometer had risen to $23,000 (in, of course, 1961 dollars). After the festival, Juliette Brewer reported that the affair had taken in $7,233.29; owing to the remarkably low overhead, the net profit was $6,269.77. The immediately important fact here was that this money could be applied to the first payment for Shakertown property.

As it happened, only ten days after Mrs. Brewer's announcement the Pleasant Hill board exercised its option on the two tracts owned by the Kurtz family, agreeing to a price of $56,000. (At one point these negotiations, which had not been easy throughout their course, became so rough that Wallace told the trustees: "Perhaps those of the committee who have not taken part in the Kurtz negotiations would be in a better position to renew [them] and continue with or without Mr. McClure's assistance.") This move meant only that Pleasant Hill was contracting to buy the property, not that it was actually handing over money, but the action should, said Jane Hutton, put fresh impetus into the local fund drive. Some people, it seemed, had been holding back, waiting to see whether the committee really meant business—but, said Miss Hutton, "a contract to buy is serious business." On December 16, in another piece of serious business, the Pleasant Hill trustees voted to exercise their option on thirty acres owned by Burwell Marshall—property that included the Centre Family House and the East Family House. This action could not really be called voluntary, however, since Marshall had sent Wallace a put-up-or-shut-up ultimatum.

Meanwhile, at a dinner that drew forty leading Lexingtonians, Wallace had announced a thirteen-day drive to raise $100,000 toward the purchase of the village. Such local notables as Fred B. Wachs, general manager of the Lexington newspapers; O. A. Bakhaus, a businessman and public official; and Emmett Milward, of the funeral home that was one of the city's oldest businesses, had offered their help, with Harry Huether, former chairman of the board of the General Telephone Company, serving as chairman of the drive and Chloe Gifford of the University of Kentucky, former president of the National Federation of Women's Clubs, heading the women's division of the campaign. Speaking at the dinner, Barry Bingham pledged full support from a Shakertown committee being formed in Louisville; Louisvillians were also being asked to put up $100,000 for the project. Just a few days earlier, Bingham had joined the Pleasant Hill board of trustees, together with Wachs, McLain, and a promising new player in the game, James L. Cogar, the former curator of Colonial Williamsburg, who had helped with the 1957 course in preservation and who was a native of the Blue Grass and a graduate of the University of Kentucky.

A month later, pushing for an ever larger board, with more citizens drawn into the action, Wallace announced the names of ten new trustees. Three were from Lexington—William H. Townsend, a lawyer widely known for his writings about Lincoln; Dr. Francis M. Massie, a surgeon; and Mrs. Clarkson Beard, a civic leader much involved in arts and education, but more came from outside Fayette County: Jane Bird Hutton and George Chinn were added from Mercer County; Mrs. William P. Caldwell and Enos Swain, editor of the *Danville Advocate,* from Boyle County; and Mrs. George W. Norton Jr. and Elbert Gary Sutcliffe from Louisville. The latter served as chairman of the Centre College board of trustees. Francis S. Hutchins, president of Berea College, rounded out the notable group.

Amid all this activity, November 4 had become a date to be preserved in the annals of Pleasant Hill. On this day, although preoccupied by fundraising efforts, the Shakertown leaders demonstrated their allegiance to Raymond McLain's principle of greater usefulness by staging their first event in the realm of ideas. This conference—"The Shaker Character: Does It Have Meaning for Today?"—brought together Edward Deming Andrews, curator of the Hancock Shaker Village at Pittsfield, Massachusetts, former professor of history at Yale, and an expert on Shaker furniture; Gerald Ham, who continued to serve Pleasant Hill as an adviser; and Captain Frank Owen, who had come from England to spend a month as consultant on education to the Shakertown project. A pioneer in residential adult education, Owen had made good use of his four years as a prisoner of war of the Japanese by developing for his fellow prisoners an educational program without benefit of books or writing materials, and since 1947 had served as principal of a residential college that he had started from scratch.

The effects of the conference do not lend themselves to easy assessment, aside from the obvious publicity value, but later comments on Pleasant Hill itself made by Owen to McLain, who was leaving again for Cairo, sounded a provocative note. "A true friend," said the captain, "would point out to you the dangers of disunity as still remaining strong and needing to be guarded against by a greater readiness to compromise on inessentials of difference. Every new project has such dangers as each of its supporters presses for aims dear to himself."

In passing Owen's words on to the board of trustees, McLain urged the members to take them to heart, and he went on: "I would add only one comment: let us not fall into the fatal trap of questioning one another's motives." Every aspect of the plan, it seemed, had its advocates—educational activities, arts and crafts, tourist attractions. "I'm afraid I am getting preachy," McLain said, "but the admonition for little children (which we all are) to 'love one another' comes as close as possible to a profound summation." More mundanely, McLain added that, since "it is necessary to *do* things together if any group is to stay together in any many-sided and long-continued project," the group had an easily chosen task before it: It must get the money to take up the options and buy the property. Otherwise, none of the discussion could have any real meaning.

McLain then went on to list what he saw as the needed practical fund-raising steps:

1. The board should set a target date for raising $100,000 (he suggested January 13, a "lucky number"); every board member should first make his own maximum gift; only then could the board then approach other prospective donors; McCallister should administer this effort—processing cards, securing progress reports from solicitors, and performing all the other necessary chores;

2. At the same time, McCallister should work with the existing solicitation efforts, with the downtown Lexington group, in Harrodsburg, and elsewhere;

3. A ruling on tax-exempt status should be secured from the IRS;

4. While taking these steps, the board should also employ a professional fund-raising firm to assume responsibility for the total campaign effort (McCallister had independently urged the same action); all experience showed, McLain said, the necessity of having professional guidance for achieving sizable financial goals—it was as necessary as professional advice for achieving the proper restoration of the property itself; counsel should be brought in immediately, to enable the mounting of a major effort to secure the entire fund.

Earl Wallace later characterized 1961 as "the beginning year" of Shakertown at Pleasant Hill, and a memorable year it had proved to be. No one could disagree with McLain's injunction about the importance of raising money, but how well his suggested approach would work and how much money would be needed remained fundamental questions—and they might well represent only the beginning.

CHAPTER VII

Fund-Raisers—
Professional and Otherwise

🌾

I n November 1961, sounding Raymond McLain's note, Ralph McCallister commented to Earl Wallace that, as it was, the Pleasant Hill fund-raising effort did not seem likely to succeed: "the methods used on the operation fund and those on the beginning of the capital fund are not adequate to the size of the undertaking." McCallister proposed the creation of a committee to study the question, and he also suggested further talks with a professional fund-raiser the group had previously consulted. Moving ahead, Wallace, who himself had no experience in philanthropic fund-raising, brought in representatives of a Pittsburgh firm, Ketchum, Inc., to survey the scene. In January, these observers produced a report that presented a mixture of question and promise.

The firm could create a successful program, said Ketchum, but the experts pointed to several aspects of the Shakertown project that would pose special problems for fund-raisers. In particular, the restoration of a village the size of Shakertown would be quite different from any restoration ever undertaken by a private group in the area—a colossal understatement—and therefore had no precedent or example of success to follow. In addition, the project had no constituency—no school, church, hospital, or other institution. Further, at this point nobody could say very clearly what was supposed to happen in Pleasant Hill beyond the opening of an inn and

restaurant and the assembling of a small exhibition of Shaker items. However, said one of the Ketchum representatives, the project had enlisted a
great many dedicated overall supporters and a number of others who had
special interest in certain phases of it, such as its attraction to tourists or the
importance of authentic preservation of the buildings. "He says," Wallace
reported to the trustees, that "we must elevate our own restrained view of
not only the quality of this undertaking, but of its potential contribution
to Kentucky."

In learning that fund-raising for historic preservation differs from all
other fund-raising efforts and requires a very special approach, Wallace and
the Shakertown trustees were recapitulating the experience of the founders
of the National Trust for Historic Preservation, who had originally imagined currents of preservationist contributions that in fact had never begun
flowing. Clearly, any preservation project would most probably have only a
nominal public constituency; the best sources of funds, as Wallace later
observed, would be "individuals of strong financial capacity and with a
particular interest in historic preservation." But what John D. Rockefeller
Jr. was likely to show up at Shakertown?

Overall, Wallace found his early fund-raising days a true learning experience. At the beginning, he said, "none of us were capable of a creditable
judgment as to the cost of the project or as to the prospect of raising adequate funds" to carry it out. Despite everything that committee members
had heard about previous efforts that had failed because of the size of the
task, "we continued to intoxicate ourselves with the idea that people 'out
yonder' with bountiful funds had only to be approached" to be won over to
this unique endeavor. "I had never been on the nonprofit side of the street
before," he said. "I had always been working for money, and here these
people were going to give it away." But his crystal ball proved to be cloudy,
indeed: "How we could have been so naive about being able to raise 'big
money' so easily as we were thinking, I will never understand." He summed
up his reflections: "No one who had headed such a major project could
have been as naive as I in thinking that people and foundations are loose
with their money for historic preservation."

How did matters work out with Ketchum and its experts? Despite
some favorable elements in their appraisal of the situation, noted Wallace,

they were badly mistaken in their judgment of the likelihood that Lexington business leaders would rush to support activities in a village as far away from the city as Pleasant Hill. Wallace also commented that Lexington was still tearing down historic buildings "to make way for commercial and industrial expansion through urban renewal."

In any case, the executive committee, in a January 30, 1962, meeting—at which the members elected Wallace chairman and Charles Sturgill, a leading Lexington car dealer, vice chairman—discussed and approved arrangements with the fund-raisers. (In accepting this post, Wallace essentially took on the role of chief executive officer of Pleasant Hill, in effect becoming the long-sought "acceptable" person "who might take" the job of running the show.) In the following weeks Ketchum staff members, working with Ralph McCallister, conducted an intensive campaign in Lexington. But, new to this game, Wallace realized as time went on that "no fund raiser representative ever talked with any prospective donor, or intended to, and we were too inexperienced in such circles to have known that fund raisers make no contacts themselves but only direct the work of others in the project from a background position." The result was that after paying the fund-raisers' fee and expenses, Shakertown realized only a few thousand dollars and a few pledges, "some of which," Wallace said mournfully, "were not honored."

An immediate need for cash arose when the expiration date approached for the option on the Trustees' House (the inn); the modern-day trustees had to come up with an immediate payment of $62,500, which they did not have. Barry Bingham came forth with a challenge offer of $25,000 if the other trustees would raise the rest of the money. "The seriousness of our undertaking dawned on me and five other trustees," Wallace said, "when we had to endorse Shakertown's note at a Lexington bank to get the balance." The transaction was made with LeRoy Miles of the First Security Bank, and since Dorothy Clay had signed first, Miles gravely warned her that, in case of default, she would be responsible for repaying the entire sum; that seems to have been the most humorous moment of the day. One member of the group commented that Shakertown would own one piece of property if it never had another. (In August, Pleasant Hill certainly looked unlikely ever to own anything else at all—Hilary Boone, the treasurer, reported that the organization had only a hundred dollars in the bank, "with many bills outstanding.")

As the year advanced and the fund-raising teams scoured Lexington for money, Wallace tried another traditional path to funding. Looking for a major gift that could get the actual restoration on its feet, he began corresponding with a number of leading foundations and, always at his own expense, undertook trips to New York, Washington, Baltimore, Cleveland, Detroit, Toledo, Chicago, Minneapolis, Akron, Canton, Wilmington, Cincinnati, Dayton, Atlanta, Houston, Battle Creek, Pittsburgh, and, closer to home, Louisville. Nobody, he reported, even went so far as to encourage him to file a formal application for a grant—even a small one—and nobody showed any confidence in Pleasant Hill's chances for success. If at least some of the restoration had already taken place, and the project thereby had some achievement to point to, perhaps money would have been a bit easier to attract. But, as it was, almost nobody in Wallace's travels had even asked him for more information about Pleasant Hill or the people involved in it. "I traveled about fifty thousand miles on airplanes to see rich people," he said, "and came back with maybe eight thousand dollars."

(Wallace stayed on the trail of outside donors, however, and in future years he would enjoy remarkable success with men and women he came to know personally, but his earlier efforts with heads of corporations brought a stack of refusals that illustrated the variety of tones the art of the kiss-off can achieve. Beginning with the basic, sweeping turndown, sometimes written by a public relations aide—"Mr. X asked me to explain that his many widespread commitments made it impossible for him to consider a personal contribution," they moved to the simple personal rejection by the tycoon himself—"While I believe your project has considerable merit, I am already overcommitted in my personal contributions this year"—to the apologetic no from the assistant—"Regrettably, the giving budget which Mr. and Mrs. X maintain is completely filled, and they will not be able to meet the request you have made of them"—to the lofty "It has been my practice for quite a few years to contribute 30% of my gross income to charity. . . . In reviewing my program I do not contemplate any changes for next year." Some begged off with deep feeling—"At present I am overwhelmed with requests from philanthropic institutions dealing with the immediate problem of the ill and injured" or "I really must ask to be excused from contributing"—while others settled for uncomplicated terseness—"I regret I will be unable to support the project to restore the Historic Village of Shakertown." The masterpiece came from an executive (and personal acquaintance) who simply returned the solicitation letter with the handwritten notation: "Earl—Sorry, I have no interest in this." Telling one executive about the array of cultural programs Pleasant Hill would present, Wallace gamely included a quote from Lewis Mumford: "A community whose life is not irrigated by art . . . is a community that exists half alive.")

As 1962 wound down, with the fund-raising executives departed and the foundations having offered neither money nor hope, Wallace found himself in something of a spot. Shakertown had made no progress in raising the money needed to begin the restoration of the Trustees' House, the only building the organization actually owned, much less in finding the funds needed to pay for the other four pieces of village property on which it held installment contracts. His Pleasant Hill colleagues had made him chairman in good part because of his general association with money, but he had presented no magic formula for funding historic preservation activities. "It was obvious that the trustees were looking to me to find enough money to begin the restoration," he noted—and this meant big money. "As chief executive I had accepted all corporate responsibilities, and my reputation and judgment were inseparably linked with the fate of the project." And, not a man to make such a statement lightly, he added, "The ultimate success of Shakertown therefore became priority number one in my affairs."

As a writer would observe some years later, "The market alone is ill-suited to protecting historically important objects and should not be entrusted with the task." But if not the market, and not foundations, and not individual Medicis and Rockefellers, and not even, it seemed, the government, then who? And how?

The seriousness of all the financial problems did not keep the Pleasant Hill team from continuing its program of activities to draw in the general public. In May 1962, Juliette Brewer and Lucy Graves, as "cochairmen" (this was, indeed, 1962), had announced that the second annual

Shakertown festival would be held September 20 through 23 (the dates were later advanced a week). In September further announcements whetted public interest in what now bore the name Pleasant Hill Autumn Festival: Governor Combs and Barry Bingham would speak; various exhibitors would show old copper, pewter, and china items, English silver, miniature furniture, and antique toys; period flower arrangements would delight visitors' eyes; and pupils from the Shakertown elementary school would appear in Shaker dress. Lucy Graves took as her own special assignment the creation of flower arrangements, which she made from wildflowers she collected along the country roads. This time, when the festival opened, it was Mrs. Brewer who removed the floral rope from the doors of the Centre Family House, with the aid of a special collaborator—Mrs. J. W. Mitchell of Danville, granddaughter of Sister Mary Settles, the schoolteacher whose death in 1923 had marked the end of the Shakers at Pleasant Hill.

Something else had changed from the opening ceremony of the previous year's festival. Now presiding was a new executive director of Pleasant Hill; the appointment of James Lowry Cogar, the former curator at Colonial Williamsburg, had been announced on June 16. After less than eleven months on the job, Ralph McCallister had gone. He had worked hard in a difficult situation—planning, speaking, writing, attending meetings of all kinds throughout Central Kentucky, and supervising the various events at Pleasant Hill, with many of these activities focused on fund-raising—but he and Pleasant Hill had not made a happy couple.

Rumbles of discontent on both sides of the situation—the executive director and the board—had led to a meeting on the afternoon of May 20, when McCallister came to see Earl Wallace to complain, first, that his position had become untenable because, while he held the responsibility for several hundred thousand dollars' worth of property, the various committees of the board had taken away his authority to administer the property, and second, that he had likewise lost the authority to administer the programs that used that property. He wanted the board either to reinstate his authority or to buy out his contract—to pay him the full balance for the remaining twenty-four months of the agreement.

Wallace was having none of this. All authority stemmed from the executive committee, he believed, which had complete control of the activities of the executive director; Wallace himself certainly had not become chairman of the executive committee in order to hand control of matters over to somebody else, whatever his title. The basic problem, Wallace noted, concerned the director's view of the role of volunteers in a project like Pleasant Hill; the problem became especially acute, Wallace commented, when "volunteers feel a superior confidence in their ability, and conversely a lack of confidence in administrative performance." The discussion in a subsequent meeting of the executive committee made plain the "existence of a great deal of friction" between McCallister and some of the committee chairmen and other board members. The director, they said, wanted to do everything himself, leaving them with little if any responsibility for executing the various projects—when, in fact, volunteers made up a vital part of the entire operation. (In saying this, the members were, from the opposite point of view, reflecting McCallister's theory of management). Some felt that the director had sometimes used poor judgment in carrying out his duties, and, worse perhaps, had "talked indiscreetly and in damaging terms about certain board members to people outside the project." "He was certainly very decided in his opinions," said Betty Morris, who, for one, got along well with him, and the fact of the matter was that "the women just didn't like him."

Overall, the members of the executive committee saw the deterioration of the relationship between McCallister and the board as so serious that his presence was "hampering the whole effort of Shakertown, Inc." But how could matters improve when the director refused "to admit being at fault in any way"? One way or another, the relationship had effectively ended, and after negotiations a deal was struck buying out McCallister.

As for the chief executive officer, Wallace himself, he was a man of great charm and even courtliness and also of marked likes and dislikes; he had a pronounced way of taking to some persons and not to others, and all the evidence suggests that McCallister fell into the negative category. Obviously, Wallace was far from alone in holding this opinion, but in any case, whatever McCallister's personal merits and deficiencies, with his particular résumé he was simply not the right person for Pleasant Hill in 1961 or 1962.

Guided by Raymond McLain's insistence on the importance of moving immediately into programs aimed at improving society, the trustees in their search for a director had looked for somebody with an executive background (obviously an important consideration here) combined with experience in program content, and McCallister came from Chautauqua, perhaps the most famous fountainhead of American popular education and cultural uplift. But in doing so, the trustees ignored the fact that they were attempting to raise money to carry out a great work of historic preservation and restoration, and that they had to restore and create the setting before they could put on any but the most limited programs. When they chose McCallister, the trustees believed that they had found a director "completely in accord with the purposes of the project," but in reality they had put the cart far in front of the horse. Any hope that a committee of McCallister's disdained amateurs could guide the actual work of preservation was simply unrealistic, even if it should include architects and other professionals. Pleasant Hill, in short, needed a preservationist to guide the work, and it needed one full time.

While the trustees busied themselves with the McCallister flap, another personnel issue had arisen in their own ranks. In January, Retta Wright, one of the most prominent and active trustees—in Boone's view the hardest worker of them all—had objected to Wallace's moving to enlarge the board by "selecting" a number of Lexington businessmen for it; as chairman of the nominating committee, she observed with some acerbity that since no names had been submitted to the committee, she did not even know who these prospective members were. Her larger complaint turned on her objection to enlarging the board to make it a fund-raising group itself instead of creating fund-raising committees, and to filling it with Lexingtonians when "foundations and large donors would feel it was a more responsible board of trustees if it was widely representative of Kentucky and included some of the special friends we have mentioned outside the state." Even if some of the new members should prove to be members of her own family, she said, she would feel compelled to vote against them. She also observed, pointedly, that "we have been ineffective for the past months and this will certainly be our last chance to save and use this village."

It seems obvious that Mrs. Wright disapproved of Wallace's executive style as well as of specific actions, and objected, as she saw it, to being ignored. Unfortunately, Raymond McLain was not on hand to soothe feelings with his spiritually oriented emollience, and the result was that Mrs. Wright resigned, as—sadly from the point of view of the origins of the project—did her sister, Lucy Graves; Dorothy Norton Clay succeeded Mrs. Wright as secretary of the board. (One person said that Wallace did not want to listen to the women on the board, yet that point seems highly questionable, since Dorothy Clay and such other stalwarts as Juliette Brewer stayed with him; later in the year, in fact, Mrs. Clay agreed to serve as administrative officer assisting the director. More likely, perhaps, was that Wallace, a fully committed and tenacious executive who "would not stop till finishing a project," as one associate said, sometimes seemed to pay little heed to others, whether women or men. Mrs. Clay, who from time to time made generous contributions of IBM stock to the cause, seems to have had no particular policy differences with Wallace, but, according to Jim Thomas, her later resignation from the board came because she objected to the chairman's "bowdlerization" of the minutes.)

Looking back at his earliest associations with Pleasant Hill, Jim Cogar remembered that when he was a small child his family would bring him on picnic excursions to nearby High Bridge. It was an all-day trip in the Model T there and back from Midway, in Woodford County, "usually consisting of five or six punctures on the way and stopping at every stream to fill the radiator." Sometimes they would have Shakertown's inn as their planned destination, but they would carry a large hamper of food in case the car couldn't quite make it that far. When they clattered into the village on the rocky and rutted Lexington-Harrodsburg Pike, young Jim would see Sister Mary Settles seated on the porch of the biggest building, the Centre Family House. "I was told that when the last Shaker died, the world was going to end," he recalled. "This disturbed me a great deal, because I was afraid that when Sister Mary died the whole universe was going to disappear. I spent a good deal of time praying for her survival."

While a student at the University of Kentucky in the late 1920s, Cogar, who clearly had already chosen his destiny, spent much of his free time scouring the Blue Grass area for antiques. After graduating with a major in history, he went off to Harvard, where he acquired his master's degree in 1929, and then to Yale for courses in architecture. In 1931 had come the opportunity to become curator at Colonial Williamsburg, where Cogar had remained to build up his fine national reputation for seventeen years, until resigning to join with partners in opening a firm dealing with the very subjects with which he had spent almost two decades—eighteenth-century furniture and furnishings. After his resignation he continued to serve as an adviser to Colonial Williamsburg, however, selecting furniture and furnishings in exhibition buildings and counseling on furnishings, paint color, and other questions in other buildings. During the ensuing years he served as furniture adviser to the American Institute of Architects (AIA) and as a consultant to a variety of preservation-related institutions and activities, including the Octagon, the headquarters of the AIA in Washington, the National Park Service, and a number of historic houses; he also supervised the furnishing of the Florida governor's new mansion in Tallahassee.

Although he had lived away from Kentucky since graduating from college, Cogar had one brush with Shakertown some eleven or twelve years later, when Burwell Marshall, the Louisville lawyer who owned part of the village and always hoped to restore it, asked whether he would consider taking on the job. Cogar turned him down, and, as described earlier, Marshall made no progress in his endeavor. In 1957 Cogar came to Lexington to take part in the Blue Grass Preservation Short Course along with the other preservationist luminaries. Then the death of one of his Williamsburg partners meant that his business would have to undergo changes, and the serious illness of his mother brought him back to Central Kentucky in 1962, perhaps only temporarily. But these events, though sad in themselves, represented a remarkable and perhaps even make-or-break stroke of luck for Pleasant Hill—especially combined, as they were, with Cogar's lifelong interest in the village. With such a star actually in the neighborhood—a man with many friends in the area, notably including Dorothy Clay—it was clearly inevitable that Earl Wallace would rush to capture him for the directorship of the project—"I must say," noted Wallace, "at a modest salary." The job also had, as one of its most marked characteristics, a highly uncertain future. But fortune smiled on Pleasant Hill that day. "We are fortunate," Wallace said in announcing the news, "to have Mr. Cogar's experience and knowledge available to us." Indeed, obtaining the services of Jim Cogar represented a notable coup for Earl Wallace and Shakertown: in this handsome gentleman with his mellow, blended Kentucky-Virginia accent, the project had acquired, along with a great measure of credibility, its themesetter and its tastemaker.

The new executive director and the Pleasant Hill board agreed on the task to be performed, and it was enormous: to restore the village to its appearance during its most flourishing years, the period from about 1835 to 1840. On the more immediate practical level, Cogar had to engage in "minor restorations and preserving what was here." Essentially, this effort would be a maintenance operation, carried out with the help of two local Mercer County craftsmen, Jackie Sanford, a painter, and Buford Parsons, a carpenter, and Sterling Linton, a groundskeeper; Cogar and Earl Wallace and Betty Morris would come over from Lexington to help out in various ways as often as their other duties permitted. "That was the beginning," Cogar said, and it was "very slow."

Looking toward the day when Pleasant Hill would be operating the inn in the Trustees' Office, Cogar got in touch with a couple who had a national reputation in the field; they could visit Pleasant Hill as consultants, he thought, and might even agree to manage the facility themselves. These friends, however, seemed to see little point at this time in becoming involved with Pleasant Hill, expressing their doubts "as to our financial position in following through with them," but they would be interested "when we had sufficient funds." Discussing this response, the board members agreed that they must "proceed with a very simple and modest beginning."

Cogar held the portfolio at Pleasant Hill of aesthetic chief; he made no claim to be a fund-raiser and had never engaged in such work. Even so, he proved to be an important individual contributor, proposing in late 1962 to forgo $3,000 of the $6,000 he was due as salary for his six months of service during the year and to have it credited to him as partial fulfillment of a donor pledge. He then suggested that the remaining $3,000 be used to buy a car that would be for his exclusive use but that would belong to Shakertown; since Charles Sturgill could make a Tempest station wagon available at cost—$2,500—the balance could go toward the director's travel expenses (it later turned out that the car would cost $3,100). The board members enthusiastically accepted Cogar's generous offer, and they also said, accurately enough, that "his continued association with Shakertown was of utmost importance, and it was agreed that terms for the future must be worked out immediately to keep him on as the Director."

Unlike the situation at Williamsburg, Cogar had to pursue his aim of creating a cameo of a previous century in the Blue Grass without the backing of a single-minded patron like John D. Rockefeller Jr. Thus things would remain "slow" at Pleasant Hill, and no significant preservation efforts could take place, until Earl Wallace managed to produce a counterpart of one kind or another for Williamsburg's billionaire godfather.

CHAPTER VIII

The Deal—I

❦

In 1960 national advertising and marketing magazines buzzed with talk
of the "soaring sixties," an alliterative new decade of national abundance and consequent rising profits for businesses of all kinds. But not
only could these forecasters have no inkling of the shape the coming years
would actually assume (nor could anyone else), they would soon be dis-
comfited by the decade's failure not only to get off to the hoped-for soaring
start but even to leave the ground. Indeed, when the Kennedy administration took office in January 1961, the U.S. economy had slid into recession.
(In Mercer County, Kentucky, in May 1960, 7.1 percent of the workers
covered by unemployment insurance were seeking jobs; in February 1961
the figure had risen to 8.2 percent, and farm workers were not included in
these statistics.)

In response, President Kennedy gave high priority to a proposed "depressed areas" bill, which represented his attempt to carry out a major promise he had made when campaigning in West Virginia and other economically
suffering states. Kennedy got off to a slow start with his legislative agenda,
but the passage of the depressed areas act in the spring represented an important victory, one of his first; he signed the act on May 1, 1961, noting that
there was "no piece of legislation which has been passed which gives me
greater pleasure to sign." With an intended appropriation of $394 million
over four years, the Area Redevelopment Administration (ARA) began operation a few weeks later; its checkbook held $200 million for commercial

and industrial loans, $100 million for other loans, $75 million for grants for public facilities, $4.5 million for technical assistance, $10 million to support job trainees, and $4.5 million for their training. The focus was on plants and other facilities in urban and low-income agricultural areas, with provision for loans to construct such infrastructure facilities as water systems. Clearly, the sponsors saw this chiefly as a smokestack act, to put new industrial jobs within the reach of people needing them, and they spoke of "gearing retraining to local job needs."

The aim, said one writer, was "to treat chronic unemployment with easy money and advice from Washington." But the money quickly proved anything but easy. Cautiously administered by William L. Batt, a veteran of federal and state government with much experience in dealing with employment problems, the program, intended to create new permanent jobs, drew heavy fire from opposed sides—from those who saw it moving too slowly and from those who believed it should not move at all because it did not represent sound national economic policy. Among its major less-philosophical problems was the complexity of procedures with which Congress had saddled it; it had to clear its projects with eight other departments and agencies, including an entrenched rival for control of job turf, the Small Business Administration (SBA), where some bureaucrats saw it as their duty to stifle this presumptuous newcomer.

After having operated for some two years, the ARA received a generally poor review from a Ford Foundation study, which concluded uncharitably that, whatever its other achievements, the agency had solved the unemployment problem for dozens of economists, financial technicians, and technical research experts. The preparation of an application for a grant or a loan involved a lengthy and complicated process, and after it reached Washington it entered what the study director called "a maze of administrative complexity." Depending on its nature and purpose, it might be referred for recommendation to any number of other agencies; the SBA got its oar in by having the responsibility for checking the financing and engineering aspects of the proposed project. The entire borrowing process, a reporter noted, could take months—not in itself an astounding fact, except that delays had led to the approval of a loan as much as a year after a community had ceased to be eligible because its economic statistics had improved.

Politically harassed and philosophically embattled, and of doubtful tenure, the agency had not proved to be what Kennedy might have had in mind, but for some few communities in 1962 and 1963 it represented the best hope they knew for economic betterment.

Near the end of 1962, the Pleasant Hill picture presented four significant features:

1. The Trustees' Office had been bought for $62,000 (and would shortly be paid for by loans), but the project had no money to restore it;
2. The project owed some $300,000 to the owners of the other four pieces of village property that had been bought;
3. The Shakertown Baptist Church still owned the old Meeting House, and Pleasant Hill had made no progress toward getting it under option;
4. No prospect existed anywhere of any large fund—any real money—with which the project could buy the property and begin restoration.

Studying this picture, Earl Wallace felt, in a moment of gloom, that perhaps he should propose that the board forget all about the great project of restoring the entire village and, since Pleasant Hill would as of January 2 own the Trustees' House, settle instead for simply mounting a "minifund" drive to restore the house as a tearoom with ten guest rooms on the upper floors. Even if such a capitulation to events looked inevitable, being forced to recommend it to the board would have represented a bitter defeat for him—the Wall Street moneyman, in the eyes of his friends and associates—and as enough contributions continued to come in from Shakertown trustees and others to keep the project alive, Wallace decided to sit on the idea.

Then, in the last executive committee meeting of the year, on December 26, Wallace told his colleagues that he had been looking into a fresh possibility. It would in fact call for Shakertown to head in a new direction, seeking money from an agency that had no interest whatever in historic preservation. Neither Wallace nor anybody else on the Pleasant Hill board seems to have been a student of federal legislation, and only recently had he learned about the existence, or at least the possible relevance to Shakertown, of the Area Redevelopment Administration. He reported that he had written a statement describing the purposes of the Pleasant Hill project, which he and Bob Houlihan, as Pleasant Hill's counsel, had then discussed with W. E. Davis, the Kentucky representative of the ARA, based in Frankfort. Houlihan had reviewed the establishing act and assured Wallace that a nonprofit corporation could apply to the ARA if the project was located in a classified distressed area—though, in fact, the restoration of Shakertown bore little resemblance to the establishment of a shirt or box factory, the kind of facility that tended to win ARA grants and loans in rural areas. If Shakertown were to get any money out of the federal government, it certainly would not come for aesthetic reasons. Encouraging his visitors, Davis had told them that the secretary of commerce had, indeed, added Mercer County to the classified list; apparently, a recent rise in unemployment had opened a window of financial opportunity. (Vivian Landrum of Harrodsburg recalled how it had pained her and others to have to call Mercer County a distressed area in order to apply for the money.) Davis agreed to forward the statement to the ARA staff in Washington; Shakertown's chances of success, he thought, were good.

(Looking in all possible funding directions, Wallace had made earlier, smaller attempts to get federal dollars, having inquired about the possibility of a loan from the Small Business Administration to pay workers when the new Shakertown Inn opened, and, shortly afterward, having asked the SBA for a loan to restore the Trustees' House to create the dining room. Nothing came of these ideas.)

Early in the new year, Wallace went off to Washington to meet with W. R. Abell, the chief financial officer of the ARA. Abell confirmed Davis's (and Houlihan's) opinion of Pleasant Hill's eligibility for funds but, as the federal funding game began, pointed out that Pleasant Hill would have to submit not one but two applications. The first, which was needed in order to establish formal eligibility, would describe the project and explain how it would be operated so as to benefit the economy of the community. The second application would consist of a feasibility report, which would justify approval of the loan on the basis that net income from operating the village would cover the loan plus interest over a period of forty years.

Though it had its complexities, the first application was, relatively speaking, a piece of cake. The second, however, would pose formidable demands for Wallace and his associates; it would be a feasibility report in every sense of the term, and would be filed with ARA's financial, engineering, and legal staff in Atlanta. It would demand a great deal of concentrated work, but that was fine with Wallace. He was prepared to make whatever case would prove to be required. Up until now, going here and there hat in hand asking for money for a good cause, he had been operating under a handicap: he had no background as a philanthropic fund-raiser and, indeed, as noted earlier, had expressed surprise at his own naiveté about the ease with which "big money" could be raised. But now, in entering upon what amounted to a protracted, high-level business negotiation involving big money, he was about to play his own game.

After acquiring his early education at what was then called Sue Bennett Memorial School, in London, Kentucky, Wallace had moved on to the University of Kentucky, graduating in 1921 with a degree in mining engineering, and had begun his career by working in Lee County as an oil geologist. Though not widely known as an oil-producing area, Lee and its neighboring counties, with their many small pools, were lively scenes of wildcatting activities and offered a good challenge to a newcomer. Wallace had worked in the oil fields of eastern and south-central Kentucky for the next seven years, and like many another person who enters that business, he spent much of his time negotiating leases and putting together deals for drilling these properties. In 1928 he had moved back to Lexington to manage the Central Kentucky affairs of the Petroleum Exploration Company, and during the 1930s he also held the position of president of the People's Gas Company of Kentucky and directed oil exploration for the Wiser Oil Company, working out of a small office off the Esplanade in downtown Lexington. Like many another oil man, as his daughter recalled, he liked to keep rock samples; they lined the window ledge and "you could smell the oil." Wallace was also president of the Kentucky Oil and Gas Association from 1934 to 1939.

After the United States entered World War II, Wallace, with his nose for oil and his experience in securing leases, left Kentucky to become land and production manager of the crude oil production division of Sohio (Standard Oil Company of Ohio), based in Cleveland. Under the demands of war, Sohio needed as much crude as could be found, and in pursuit of it Wallace scoured the South and parts of Latin America, from Guatemala to Venezuela, acquiring the leases and setting up the combinations needed to obtain this vital commodity for Sohio. He soon became a vice president of the company.

Thus Wallace, as both engineer and businessman, developed through the years what might be called a subject-matter specialty—oil—and a functional specialty—the making of arrangements to exploit the oil properties that were found. It was, therefore, not altogether surprising that in the early 1950s he moved from Sohio to Wall Street, nor should his choice of an investment banking house in general and of Dillon, Read and Company in particular as his new business home have surprised anyone who took a close look. In retrospect, one particular detail about his years in Cleveland should not surprise anybody either: fate saw to it that he lived in Shaker Heights.

Although financial firms have many features in common, they also differ almost as if they were individual persons. Of the two principal types of Wall Street activities, stock trading and investment banking, the latter clearly fitted Wallace, with its focus on putting packages together to raise funds for client companies and its emphasis not on the ups and downs of the moment but on relationships, probity, and planning for long periods of time.

Since the 1890s, Dillon Read (under its various names) had moved on from the older investment banking practice of taking part in successive underwritings of corporate bond issues as a middleman—going from one project to the next—and instead had devoted much of its effort first to putting a structure together and then to staying with the resulting entity, assisting it in building its operations. This careful, long-term approach, which had acquired the name "relationship banking," had become characteristic of Dillon Read; the firm had applied it so thoroughly at times that once, for instance, it even found itself running a large automobile company, Dodge, before selling it to Chrysler.

In the 1930s, Dillon Read had moved into a field new to it, natural gas transmission, arranging the first significant private placement of a U.S. pipeline company's bonds. After the war, in the largest corporate underwriting since the 1929 crash, the firm took over the privatization of the famous Big Inch and Little Big Inch oil transmission lines, which, in a special form of World War II antisubmarine warfare, the government had built to move oil from the southwestern fields to the Northeast. This step made Dillon Read a major player in the oil and gas industries, for which, as one market analyst noted, it soon became known for developing "imaginative financing." (In the pre-Enron era, this description did not imply chicanery.)

The structure dreamed up for financing Union Oil of California provides a striking but typical example. After the war this company had begun a large-scale program of oil exploration that required large amounts of capital. How could Dillon Read help? The firm produced an innovative response; it would organize a Dillon Read subsidiary called Nassau Associates, which would hire petroleum engineers to estimate the production to be expected in a Union Oil field. Nassau would then draw up estimates of the value of the oil over the life of the field and would contract to buy a portion of that production.

Next Nassau (that is, Dillon Read) would create two companies, "A" and "B," whose securities would be sold to investors. The "A" securities were actually bonds, although not so termed, because they had first call on income; unless the engineers turned out to have been crazy or the bottom dropped out of the oil market, "A" investors were bound to make money. "B" investors held stock in the company, which conferred ownership like any other common stock; in some deals a person buying "A" paper would also receive "B" shares as an inducement—a kind of bonus. Nassau would sell the production contract to a large investor, such as an insurance company, retaining a one-quarter interest in both "A" and "B" companies and selling the other three-quarters to investors.

Such was the challenging context into which, in 1953, stepped Earl Wallace, a veteran of more than thirty years' experience linking oil and finance. In this world of long-term and sophisticated dealings he would arrange mergers, "putting together oil companies and oil properties," as his daughter described it; not simply a moneyman, as many of his Lexington friends may have regarded him, he was, in fact, a specialist—a dealmeister who had now taken up residence in a house of deals, among men who, as one observer said, "enjoyed the hunt." A decade later, for all its own troubles and all the problems it could create for others, the Area Redevelopment Administration could prove exasperating to such a man but it could hardly overawe him.

W. E. Davis, the ARA representative in Frankfort, had suggested to Wallace that Shakertown might qualify for both a grant and a loan; the loan would go toward paying for the cost of restoration, while the grant would cover nonrevenue-producing facilities, such as service roads, utilities, fencing, and parking lots. Wallace originally put the total amount to be requested at $1,250,000, with the grant coming to $250,000. With respect to the loan, which was seen as obtainable at 4 percent over twenty-five years, Wallace and his consultants would have to create projections of yearly revenues to demonstrate that Shakertown could pay the money back. Before long, these figures had changed; Wallace now sought a total of $2 million, with $400,000 of it in a grant. This higher figure came from A. Edwin Kendrew, senior vice president and architectural director of Colonial Williamsburg, who visited Pleasant Hill at Wallace's request to make an estimate of the cost of restoring the village; Kendrew's figure, Wallace noted, came as a "shock." (As well it might; the amount in 2005 would be perhaps six times as much.)

To qualify for an ARA loan, Shakertown would need to employ a registered architect, who would produce a master plan for the restoration, with drawings and projections of costs, and would certify that the buildings could be restored and put to the uses as described. The project would also require the services of an engineering firm to survey the property and design a mechanical plan. But meeting these preliminary requirements would cost about $10,000, much more money than Shakertown had available to spend on anything. (Hilary Boone's treasurer's report for April showed that, aside from money earmarked for repayment of the note at the First Security National Bank, Shakertown at Pleasant Hill had a cash balance of precisely $16.57.) Without these plans there would be no loan, and thus it

Dr. Francis Pennebaker, standing; Sisters Sarah Pennebaker and Mary McGaughey, seated on chairs; and Sisters Mary Petters, Lula Harris, and Cynthia Shain, seated on steps. Courtesy of the University of Kentucky Libraries.

Blacksmith's Shop, 1815 (later the Carpenter's Shop and, still later, the Broom Shop), before restoration, north view. Courtesy of the Wallace family collection and the University of Kentucky Libraries.

Renovation of the Centre Family Dwelling, before restoration, west side view. Courtesy of the Wallace family collection and the University of Kentucky Libraries.

Old Ministry's Workshop, 1812, before restoration, north side view. Courtesy of the Wallace family collection and the University of Kentucky Libraries.

(*Above*) East Family Dwelling, before restoration, west side view. Courtesy of the Wallace family collection and the University of Kentucky Libraries. (*Below*) West Family Wash House (left), 1842, Preserve Shop (middle), 1859, and West Family Sisters' Shop (right), 1845. Courtesy of the University of Kentucky Libraries.

(*Above*) Joseph Graves Sr., a Lexington businessman, spearheaded the first efforts to save Shakertown. Courtesy of the Graves family collection.

(*Left*) Jane Bird Hutton, editor and publisher of the *Harrodsburg Herald*, stressed economic benefits of the restoration. Courtesy of the *Harrodsburg Herald*.

Barry Bingham Sr., editor and publisher of the Louisville *Courier-Journal*, promoted restoration, recruited friends, and donated money to buy the Trustees' Office. Courtesy of the *Courier-Journal*.

Charles Graves (left), dean of the University of Kentucky School of Architecture; Chairman Earl D. Wallace (center); and Wallace Taylor (right), architect for phase one of the restoration. Courtesy of the Wallace family collection and the University of Kentucky Libraries.

Centre Family House. Courtesy of the Wallace family collection and the University of Kentucky Libraries.

During a ceremony at the second annual Shakertown Festival, Governor Bert Combs was presented a book written by D. M. Hutton on Shaker history by trustee Dorothy (Mrs. John Harris) Clay of Paris. (*Harrodsburg Herald* photo, September 1962). Courtesy of the University of Kentucky Libraries.

Centre Family Dwelling restoration, 1973, west elevation with scaffolding. Bill Trumbo is on the scaffold and Henry Higgins is on the ground. Courtesy of the Wallace family collection and the University of Kentucky Libraries.

April 1970, Cooper's Shop, west elevation. Carpenters are installing a pent entrance to the cellar. Courtesy of the Wallace family collection and the University of Kentucky Libraries.

(*Above*) September 1966, Ministry's Workshop, north and west view during the restoration. Note the nonconforming shed being moved away from side of the building. Courtesy of the Wallace family collection and the University of Kentucky Libraries. (*Below*) The basement of the Carpenter's Shop, 1815, during the restoration. Courtesy of the Wallace family collection and the University of Kentucky Libraries.

Jackie Sanford (left) and Cornell Powell (right), head of the restoration crew. Photo was taken in the mid-1960s during the making of reproduction Shaker furniture to be used in public areas and guest rooms. Courtesy of the Wallace family collection and the University of Kentucky Libraries.

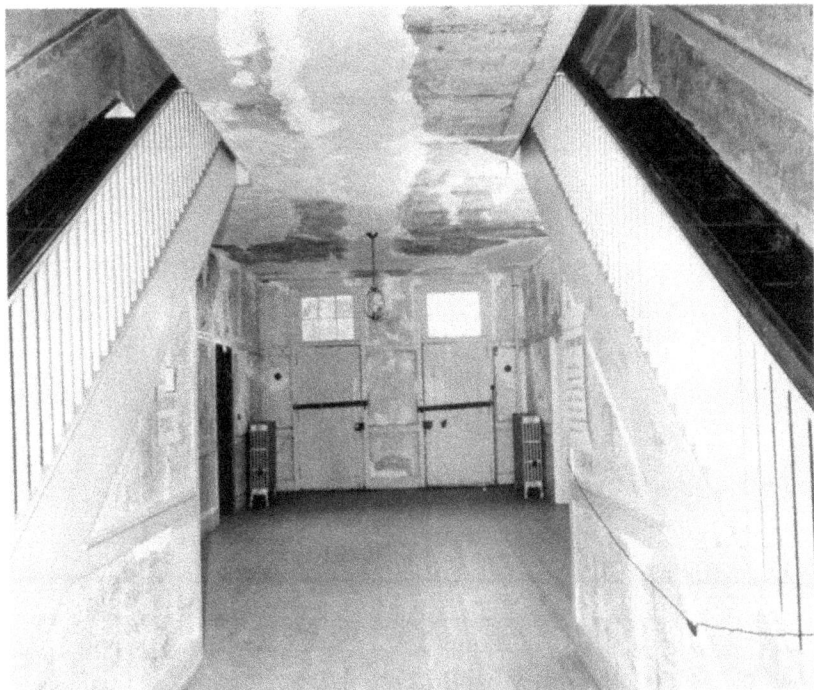

(*Above*) The front hall of the East Family Dwelling, looking south. Courtesy of the Wallace family collection and the University of Kentucky Libraries. (*Below*) Main Street of the village, looking west. Modern paved road Highway 68 was removed in 1967 during the restoration. Courtesy of the University of Kentucky Libraries.

(*Above*) The Water House, designed and constructed by Micajah Burnett in 1833. Courtesy of the University of Kentucky Libraries. (*Below*) The East Family Dwelling, 1817. The door opening faces the East Family Sisters' Shop, 1855. Courtesy of the University of Kentucky Libraries.

(*Above*) The Trustees' Office, 1839, where Shakers did business with the world. It also served as a hotel. Courtesy of the University of Kentucky Libraries.

(*Right*) The entrance to the Trustees' Office, 1839, which shows a Federal fanlight detail with side lights. Fine Flemish bond brickwork is evident in this photograph. Courtesy of the University of Kentucky Libraries.

(*Above*) West side view of the Trustees' Office showing main block and ell to the right. The Ministry's Workshop, 1821, is in view in right of photograph. Courtesy of the University of Kentucky Libraries. (*Below*) View of the front elevation of the Centre Family Dwelling before restoration. Brethren entered through the right side door and Sisters through the left. Courtesy of the University of Kentucky Libraries.

(*Above*) The dining room of the Centre Family Dwelling after restoration. Courtesy of the University of Kentucky Libraries.

(*Left*) The apothecary exhibit in the Centre Family Dwelling. Courtesy of the University of Kentucky Libraries.

Secretary of the Interior Rogers C. B. Morton (left) and Earl D. Wallace (right) at the Historic Landmark dedication for Shakertown. Courtesy of the University of Kentucky Libraries.

Shakertown officers receive a national tourism award from the Society of American Travel Writers (left to right): Earl D. Wallace; Ralph Dunlop, president of the Society of American Travel Writers; Dorothy Norton Clay; and James L. Cogar. Courtesy of the Wallace family collection and the University of Kentucky Libraries.

An early Christmas celebration during the restoration; everyone is wearing Shaker attire (left to right): Betty W. Morris,
director of hotel operations; James L. Cogar, retired president;
Elizabeth C. Kremer, director of food; and James C. Thomas,
president. Courtesy of the Wallace family collection and the
University of Kentucky Libraries.

John Harris and Dorothy
Clay (left) join Joseph and
Lucy Graves (right) for
the Viennese ball. They
helped organize local
preservationists. Courtesy
of the Graves family
collection.

James L. Cogar. Courtesy of the Wallace family collection and the University of Kentucky Libraries.

Margaret "Retta" Wright, sister of Lucy (Mrs. Joseph) Graves, recruited volunteers. Courtesy of the Graves family collection.

Robert Jewell was a Wilmore, Kentucky, farmer and an early Shakertown trustee. Courtesy of the Jewell family collection.

Attorney Robert Houlihan Sr., the secretary of trustees, drafted early legal papers incorporating Shaker Village at Pleasant Hill. Courtesy of Robert F. Houlihan Jr.

Hilary Boone Jr. sought funding and leaders with restoration expertise. Courtesy of Hilary Johnson Boone.

Robert Brewer of Lexington, who chaired the farm committee, was the son of Juliette (Mrs. Lawrence) Brewer. Courtesy of the Brewer family collection.

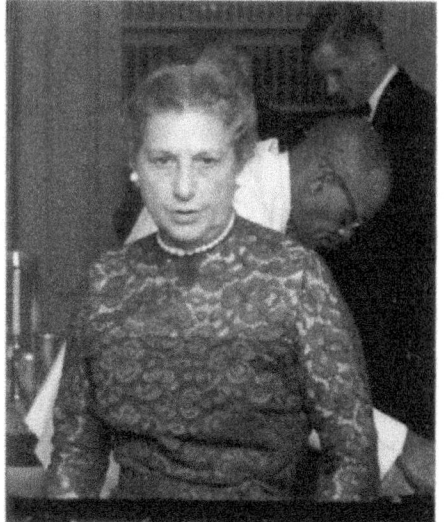

Juliette (Mrs. Lawrence) Brewer was a notable champion of preservation causes. Courtesy of the Brewer family collection.

Board officers after death of Earl D. Wallace (left to right): William T. Young, chair; Alex G. Campbell Jr., vice chair; Richard C. Stephenson, secretary; and Robert L. Warren, treasurer. Courtesy of Shaker Village of Pleasant Hill.

Gulf Stream Park Track in Florida. Three friends, trustees, and benefactors of Shakertown (left to right): Alex G. Campbell Jr., Sally (Mrs. W. Lyons) Brown of Louisville, and William T. Young. Courtesy of the Young family collection.

William T. Young (left) and Alex G. Campbell Jr. (right) at Young's plantation, Mercer Mill, near Albany, Georgia. Close friends Campbell and Young were picked by Earl Wallace to serve on the Shakertown board in 1985. Courtesy of the Young family collection.

William T. Young (left) and Alex G. Campbell Jr. (right) at the Kentucky Derby at Churchill Downs in the early 1990s. Courtesy of the Young family collection.

Philip Davidson, former University of Louisville president, became an educational consultant to the Shakertown Roundtable. Courtesy of the *Courier-Journal*.

Albert (Al) Smith (left), trustee and chairman of the Shakertown Roundtable, and Alexander Heard (right), Chancellor Emeritus of Vanderbilt University, who chaired the Roundtable conference on higher education. Courtesy of Albert Smith.

Madge Adams and Jim Thomas. Adams succeeded Thomas as president and CEO on May 1, 2005. Courtesy of the Shaker Village of Pleasant Hill.

looked for a time as if the whole enterprise might collapse for want of $10,000. The situation was saved by one of the trustees, Elbert Gary Sutcliffe, chairman of the Centre College board, who offered Shakertown the $10,000 in a no-interest loan.

Turning to friends of Jim Cogar's at Williamsburg, Wallace received from Kendrew the names of the only five restoration architects in the United States deemed worthy of being considered for the project. From the list Wallace chose Washington Reed, who practiced in Warrenton, Virginia, but had formerly been at Williamsburg and was himself a friend of Cogar's. Reed's endorsement by Williamsburg and Wallace's assurance that he would be properly registered to practice in Kentucky well before he had to sign off on the plans won him ready approval from ARA officials. Reed having agreed to come to Shakertown on a per diem basis as needed, he and Cogar were now set to begin developing the required master plan for the restoration. Although these moves had been dictated by ARA requirements, Wallace later paid tribute to their value to the project. The need to develop the master plan, he said, "forced an early consensus on what we wanted the village to be, and on how far we were willing to commercialize the operations and still preserve the authenticity of the restoration." Thus, at a time in which preservation was still feeling its way nationally, Cogar, together with Reed, had as his first major task the creation of a concept to guide the work of restoration. He developed the "adaptive usage" plan, a combination of aethetics and practicality, which would aim at returning the exteriors of the buildings to their nineteenth-century appearance while turning the interiors into guest rooms and other facilities that could produce needed income for Pleasant Hill. Cogar's instructions called for him to plan for about sixty rooms for overnight guests, dining rooms in the Trustees' House, a collection of Shaker exhibits, and a gift shop. Thus was established Pleasant Hill's balance of preservation and commercialization.

Early in the ARA negotiations, Wallace had received something of a jolt when he explained to Bill Abell his plan to hire local Mercer County mechanics and laborers to do the restoration construction work, under Cogar's supervision; he foresaw perhaps twenty-five men working full-time for a period of thirty months. Abell, however, rapidly told Wallace some facts of life that made it impossible to follow this appealing plan. Government regulations required that all construction be subject to competitive bidding, and each bidder had to agree to comply with the conditions of the Davis-Bacon "prevailing wage" act, which meant that urban union labor rates would apply on this project in rural, high-unemployment Mercer County; thus high-wage, experienced workers from Louisville and Lexington would get the jobs, working as employees of subcontractors. In addition, Wallace learned to his dismay that a general contractor, chosen through bidding, would supervise the work of the subcontractors, and an architect serving as project manager would officially represent Shakertown. Cogar, who had studied architecture but had no license, would hence have no supervisory authority over the actual work itself—nor, for that matter, would Wallace. To him, the worst thing about the bidding process was that the low bidder got the job, "regardless of his competence or past experience." But that was part of the price demanded for a dance with the government. Though Wallace had no choice but to accept this price, it always rankled him.

By midsummer, architecture students from the University of Kentucky had measured all the buildings in the village, Cogar and Reed had completed the floor plans of the buildings, and Reed and J. Stephen Watkins, the consulting engineer, had certified the preliminary restoration plans. It was the completion of these steps that actually won the project a ruling of eligibility for funds (i.e., for consideration for funding, depending on the fate of the feasibility report).

Since the soundness and the persuasiveness of the feasibility report held the keys to the ARA's vault, Wallace—naturally—approached its preparation "in a way not too unlike that of a Wall Street prospectus for a public bond issue." He saw one important difference, however: Shakertown had no past record or history of operations to entice purchasers or, in this case, lenders. To support his projections of the cash flow that would be available to pay off the loan, he therefore decided to use facts and figures from other operations similar to what was proposed for Pleasant Hill; in particular, he spent several days studying the operation at Old Sturbridge Village in Massachusetts.

Old Sturbridge presented an encouraging picture, with attendance growing from year to year, and having doubled in the past six years. Visitors were spending a total of about $3 a person (1963 dollars), producing a very satisfactory cash flow. Wallace found special encouragement in the success of Sturbridge, he noted trenchantly, because that project had been started "with one old building on an otherwise bare tract" of land; it was, indeed, an artificially assembled village, lacking "the advantage of starting with a landmark of historic significance such as the original buildings and countryside at Shakertown at Pleasant Hill." In addition to his own conclusions, reached after analyzing the past ten years of Sturbridge ticket sales, Wallace enlisted the help of John Auchmoody, the financial vice president of Old Sturbridge, who came to Kentucky, examined the scene, and gave Wallace's report a full endorsement.

Since Old Sturbridge did not offer lodging and leased its lunchtime food-service operation, Wallace turned for more information to Berea College's famous Boone Tavern hotel, studying its record for the past ten years and concentrating on the cost of food per meal, the cost of preparing it, and the cost of serving it (the last figure had to be an estimate, since students provided the service). From this research he put together, prospectus style, a set of assumptions on which he based a projection of revenue and expense—in constant dollars—for ten years, showing the village's cash flow (operating cash income less cash outgo for operations) after completion of the restoration. This study, devised under the government's loan formula, indicated that a loan of $2 million would be justified.

Wallace included in his supporting evidence the attendance figures for other attractions in Central Kentucky, especially the horse farms around Lexington (125,000 visitors in 1962), Fort Harrod, and My Old Kentucky Home (100,000 each), and stressed Shakertown's strategic location just twenty-four miles south of the intersection of Interstate Highways 75 and 64 (the latter point amounting to a no-doubt permissible bit of application exaggeration of the kind familiar to anybody who has ever sought government funds, since Wallace had earlier cited the distance of Shakertown from Lexington [where the highways intersect] as a reason for the lackluster results of attempts to raise money from Lexington business interests).

Speaking to the point that most specifically concerned the ARA, Wallace

summed up the project's contribution to economic activity and employment opportunities as:

1. Immediate additional purchasing power from construction
   payrolls through two and one-half years [though, owing to the
   government's own stipulations, most of these wages would not go
   to Mercer Countians; workers would, however, spend some
   money in the county];
2. Rapid increase after the first year in permanent operating
   employment payrolls as the construction payroll phased out;
3. Rapid build-up after the first year of purchasing power brought in
   by tourists;
4. Indirect employment by others of people required to deliver goods
   and services to the village, and to bring tourist groups by bus and
   otherwise to the village;
5. Complementing the other tourist attractions in the area by
   appealing to an additional segment of the traveling public
   interested in historic preservation, especially major and unique
   types such as Shakertown.

Employment in operations would range from the night watchman to the
accountant. Wallace estimated the new purchasing power brought to the
area by payrolls and tourists at $600,000 the first year, rising to more than
$1 million in the sixth year. All of this material—and a great deal more—
buttressed by appropriate financial charts, went off to the ARA.

In April, the chairman reported a very significant bureaucratic development to the trustees: the ARA had assigned a project number to the
application. At the same time, officials had decided to weigh the application under Section 7 of the act, providing for a forty-year loan at 3.5 percent interest, instead of Section 6, which called for a twenty-five-year loan
at 4 percent; Wallace had immediately wired his assent, while noting that
the analysts would be "constructively critical" of the application and would
now want a good deal more information that had not been needed for
Section 6 but would apply to Section 7.

In a bit of the standard gamesmanship that is supposed to help applicants in their dealings with federal agencies, various board members were contacting senators and congressmen to ask for their support. The very well-connected Dorothy Norton Clay had written to Senator John Sherman Cooper and Senator Thruston Morton, both of whom had dutifully replied with expressions of interest in the project; Charlie Sturgill had written to Representative Frank Chelf of Lebanon, whose district included Pleasant Hill; and Dr. Massie offered to contact Representative John C. Watts, who lived in nearby Nicholasville.

Tom McCaskey, one of the many Williamsburg executives who freely offered advice and practical help to Shakertown, armed Wallace with some attractive summary points to use in sessions with the ARA review team in Atlanta:

> With the loan from the Area Redevelopment Administration, Shaker Village at Pleasant Hill will develop into a full-fledged travel attraction. As an outdoor museum dedicated to interpreting a way of life, it will recall a segment of the American heritage which contributed significantly to the expansion of our young nation. It will then be able to illustrate graphically the achievements of those remarkable people known as Shakers by restoring aspects of their life and customs, industry and stern dedication to principle which produced in Kentucky a type of community which held promises of Utopia.
>
> Creation of a practical, well-based and profitable operation which will result in new job opportunities in Mercer County on a long-term basis is the economic aim of the project. In order to develop the income required, Shaker Village will employ many well-tested elements of tourism. It will be basically an educational project and learning will therefore be its primary object. More elementary appeals, however, must also be employed. Satisfaction of natural curiosity, the universal yearning for something different, something unusual, entertainment elements, photographic and shopping motivations, good food in the manner of "another time," unique accommodations—all of these will be a part of Shaker Village at Pleasant Hill when plans for Phase One of its development into a travel attraction of national appeal are completed.

In concluding his thoughts, McCaskey looked forward to Phase Two of the project, when he saw the village contribution to the economic well-being of Mercer County and Kentucky increasing, with "cultural conferences, seminars and forums on art, antiques, history, science, religion and almost any educational subject." He saw Shaker Village becoming "a center of culture and intellectual stimulation which should benefit the area, state and nation."

Amid the swirl of high-level discussions, and despite the near-nonexistence of a Pleasant Hill bank balance, Jim Cogar reported to the board that the village would open to the public on May 1; visitors would be asked to pay a dollar to visit the Trustees' House and the Centre Family House. In the latter building they could see a special exhibition on Shaker life and culture created by Peter A. G. Brown, another of the helpful friends from Colonial Williamsburg, where he was director of presentation services: "They Lifted Their Hands to Work and Their Hearts to God." They needed a hostess at each building, Cogar said, and it would also be nice to have a janitor who could clean both buildings and, in his spare time, help the carpenters with their work. Cogar's friends described him as an optimist by nature, and his consistent focus on the task ahead, money in the bank or not, certainly confirmed that reading of his character.

Later in the year, two representatives from the ARA office in Atlanta, Charlie Dixon and Jack Ingram, came to Pleasant Hill with some tough questions in mind, relating particularly to projected income. They expressed strong misgivings about the effect the traffic on Highway 68 would have on the volume of visitors; the danger to pedestrians posed by cars, trucks, and buses dashing through the village, they feared, would hold down the crowds. Besides, how could the project raise the projected revenue from ticket sales with a public highway running through the middle of the village? Since Shakertown, Inc., did not at this time own the surrounding land, the analysts also noted negatively that outside business interests could open commercial businesses on privately owned land within a few hundred feet of Shaker buildings on three sides of the village, thus detracting from the appearance of the restoration and competing directly for income from the tourists. Fortunately, the Shakertown board had plans to deal with both problems.

The team from Atlanta also provided a bit of inadvertent comic relief. Faithfully following the admonition of the ARA act that forbade the extending of aid until a project seeking funds had explored all other sources, the analysts reviewed Shakertown's previous efforts to raise money. This was one point Wallace and his associates could address with absolute conviction, and the visitors apparently did not require much persuasion that they, and the ARA, truly represented Shakertown's financial last resort.

To answer the analysts' question about local support for the project—was it merely the pet scheme of an elite group interested in historic preservation or did it enjoy wide public backing?—the Shakertown group called a public meeting at the Imperial House (now the Kentucky Inn) in Lexington. Some fifty persons turned out, including a number from Louisville and Harrodsburg, and after an hour's discussion Fred Wachs, publisher of the Lexington newspapers, asked the representatives to give the group a candid estimate of Shakertown's chances of getting the loan. One of the visitors replied with the good news that they would recommend a sizable loan and that Shakertown should expect the recommendation to win approval. No money would come as a direct grant, however, because the ARA's grant funds had by now been exhausted.

During this year that featured much discussion of money but not the actual presence of very much of it, the Shakertown trustees held out the hope of a grant from Governor Combs that could keep the project in business. Combs later recalled that when Wallace, Sturgill, and other board members came to see him, they declared that Shakertown "needed a gesture—at least $50,000—to convince people that this project had the support of the people of the state and the officials of the state." Although sympathetically inclined, the governor felt limited by a constitutional provision prohibiting the use of state funds for a nongovernmental activity, and he turned his visitors down. But "they were back in about ten days, knocking on the door again." Known for his view that the purpose of a legal adviser was to tell him how to do what he had already decided to do, Combs had asked the attorney general, John Breckinridge, to solve the problem. Though in later years Wallace and the other trustees who made the request to Combs liked to joke about the governor's readiness to support them whatever the constitution said, Combs in actuality proceeded with great caution until the last days of his term, in December, when, with Breckinridge's approval, he allocated $50,000 from his emergency fund to give Shakertown its much-needed transfusion.

"That fifty thousand from Bert saved the bacon," Wallace recalled, because it enabled Shakertown, Inc., to fulfill its agreements concerning the property on the north side of Highway 68, with seventeen of the original Shaker buildings. The governor left a public reception in his honor in the capitol rotunda for a brief presentation ceremony in his executive suite. In return for the check, Wallace presented Combs with a certificate giving him and his wife lifetime admission to the village. (Combs's successor, Ned Breathitt, may have been somewhat less than thrilled by the governor's largesse, since the money might otherwise have gone toward the hiring of urgently needed prison workers—though Combs commented that the question needed more study.) Shakertown representatives reported at the time that in the first six months since the two buildings were opened on May 1, attendance had totaled 10,543, with people from every state except Montana, and seventeen foreign countries. This record had come purely from the intrinsic attraction of Pleasant Hill itself, since no actual restoration had yet taken place.

A week after New Year's, 1964, came the biggest news since the Shakertown project had begun. On January 7 the Commerce Department approved the application for a $2 million loan for the restoration of the village; the money, said the announcement, was "intended to create a tourist attraction that will provide 289 new jobs and draw 150,000 tourists a year by 1970." By time-honored custom, under which the funding of a project is always announced by the local member of Congress, regardless of whether this person approves or disapproves of the transaction or has even heard of it, the news of this federal bounty came from the office of the local congressman, Frank Chelf, who did in fact approve of it; the congressman himself telephoned Jane Bird Hutton at the *Harrodsburg Herald* with the good tidings. A few days later an editorial in the *Courier-Journal* praised the ARA for making this loan: "The money will cover every aspect of a perfect restoration." The Shakers, observed the editorial, "though highly religious, were also shrewd business men and women. They would have approved of the expert planning that is going into the restoration of their little world at Pleasant Hill. They would have liked such meticulous care for detail."

Though the *Courier-Journal* declared that this news meant that the future of Shakertown as a major tourist attraction for Kentucky was assured, newspaper readers (and perhaps the writer of the editorial as well) did not know that the federal treasury had not actually written any checks to Shakertown. What Wallace and his colleagues really had was a hunting license, entitling them to find a bank loan if they could; more precisely, since no actual transaction had yet taken place, they had only the promise of a hunting license. Typically with such a project, the government would provide funding by buying first-mortgage bonds that it would later sell to private investors, and that was what the ARA proposed to do with Shakertown. But Wallace, the expert in funding enterprises through bond issues, raised objections. If Shakertown later ran into financial problems and defaulted, any bond-holder could foreclose, and the project would have to go into receivership, with incalculable results, including loss of any control over its own destiny. Hence the problem Wallace faced before entering into a formal contract with the government involved finding a way to keep Shakertown from having to create a bond issue.

Finally, the government agreed to take a note for $2 million, secured by a first mortgage on the village property and everything on or in it, down to the cups and saucers, and on all property to be acquired within the 120-acre village area, even including the Meeting House then still owned by the Shakertown Baptist Church. The interest rate was fixed at $3\,5/8$ percent, with payments stretching over forty years. Thus Wallace had achieved what he not only wanted but considered absolutely essential: the change from the usual method of financing meant that in case of default Shakertown would always be dealing with the government and not with third parties. Third-party investors, concerned only about the income from their investments, would hardly hold back from drastic action in case of trouble; on the other hand, the government, Wallace felt, would hesitate before putting such a project out of business. Was Wallace simply practicing prudence, trying to cover an important contingency, or did he really consider a default likely? He put the answer very neatly: "I was thinking that we might renegotiate the loan if we ran into financial difficulties in the future."

Under the contract, the government did not have to advance any money until Shakertown, Inc., had completed the restoration, government inspectors had approved it, and government auditors had blessed the expenditures. What if the inspectors decided that some part of the work as carried out failed to conform to the approved plans? It was a good question, and one any banker would be quick to ask—and bankers came into the picture because the government instructed Shakertown to pledge the contract to a bank as security for a loan of $2 million; that was the only way the project would get the money.

The whole thing looked like such a bad credit risk, Wallace later observed, that complying with the conditions seemed impossible. What banker would do it? Nevertheless, he went hunting. Since at that time all of the banks in Lexington combined could not have lent as much as $2 million to one customer, he went to Louisville to talk the matter over with his friend Henry Offutt, chairman of the First National Bank. Wallace had been in touch with Offutt from time to time, keeping the banker informed about his efforts to find a big-money sponsor for the restoration and his series of failures in this quest. And, fortunately, Offutt had a strong interest in historic preservation. Yet he was the head of a bank, not a hobbyist, and Wallace himself later commented that if *he* had been a member of Offutt's board, he would have opposed making such a risky loan.

Offutt called in his senior vice president, Hubbard Buckner, and described Wallace's proposition. "Hub didn't say yes," Wallace recalled. "He just nodded." That nod confirmed Offutt's own view, and despite Wallace's no doubt unspoken qualms the bankers agreed to provide the money. "I would have to say," Wallace observed, "that Mr. Offutt had never made a shakier loan and had he not had the authority to make loans up to $2 million, the line of credit probably would have been rejected at a formal bank board meeting."

The loan constituted "an unusual show of confidence for which Shakertown has always been grateful. If First National had declined, I feel quite sure that other banks would have done likewise." As worked out in April, the deal called for the bank to lend Shakertown $2 million for a period of two years at 5½ percent interest, with the interest coming out of the $2 million. Since Wallace expected the restoration to be completed within two years, at the end of this period the ARA (which had come to the end of its three-year span and had now become the Economic Development Administration [EDA]) would pay the bank the $2 million and take over the loan at the agreed rate of 3⅝ percent for forty years.

Beyond agreeing to change the method of funding, the government during the negotiations had made two other important concessions to Shakertown. At Wallace's request, the officials agreed to allow the project to take $80,000 of the loan to furnish the buildings in Shaker style, as sought by Jim Cogar; with this money he could supervise the production of some fourteen hundred pieces of reproduced Shaker furniture and could acquire from Kentucky weavers several thousand yards of hand-loomed curtains and carpets. In agreeing to this proposal, the EDA was displaying a cooperative spirit, indeed, because it involved a departure from the generally mandatory practice of taking sealed bids for every activity. In another major concession, the government officials approved the use of some $289,000 of the money to complete the purchase of the remaining four tracts of land in the village.

Thus, though contingencies would arise in the future, for now the loan package was complete. Wallace had seized the opportunity to play his game; he had played it patiently, cleverly, and stubbornly, and he had won the prize. "He got it," said Betty Morris, "by sheer willpower." The creation of the government loan constituted the central fact in the restoration of the village. After three perilously lean years, Shakertown at Pleasant Hill, Inc., was saved, and for his earlier labors topped by this past year of effort, Wallace would be named Kentuckian of the Year by the Kentucky Press Association.

CHAPTER IX

"*A* Fantastic *Accomplishment*"

❦

O n May 31, 1964, two prominent friends of Pleasant Hill spoke at
a ceremony marking the official beginning of the restoration.
Bert Combs, who had now become a former governor, told the
crowd of about two hundred that "the history of Shakertown can be used
as a guide to help us build a progressive Kentucky." People today had much
to learn from the Shakers, Combs said, praising them for their industry,
sobriety, fairness, cleanliness, and—in a limp attempt at a joke—for their
belief that "women should stay silent unless they had something useful to
say"; the remark came as a particularly odd comment from an experienced
politician on a movement founded by a woman and governed by women
in parity with men. Moving on to firmer ground, the former governor
added an interesting specific item to the list of Shaker inventions, crediting
the Believers with dreaming up the needle with one eye.

Raymond McLain struck the note that had characterized all his contributions to discussions about Pleasant Hill. The restored village would be "a
key to serenity in the midst of the rush and demand that is constantly upon
us." Shakertown would become a retreat in which people of the present
day could absorb the values that brought the settlement into existence
(though, one might add, not all of the Shaker values, perhaps). Guests at
the village could see "life pared of its superficialities, yet see that it can
remain beautiful because it is strong and neat and not gaudy." A few days
afterward, Jim Cogar would express similar thoughts, telling a questioner:

"The whole idea is to make it a cultural and educational center." Though the village would offer visitors a beautiful experience and a fascinating look into a strange part of Kentucky's past, Cogar expressed the hope that Pleasant Hill would win its greatest fame as a quiet place to solve the world's problems.

At the opening ceremony, forty hostesses guided visitors through the buildings, which, along with a show of paintings by the Kentucky impressionist Paul Sawyier, featured a display of sturdy, functional Shaker-style tables and chairs. This furniture-making project started slowly, Cogar said, but it was about to pick up under the supervision of a new staff member, James Thomas, who had just come to Pleasant Hill. With the $80,000 made available from the EDA loan, Thomas had the particular responsibility of outfitting the buildings, making the needed furniture and accessories. "I trained some craftsmen that worked in a nonconforming building, since torn down," Thomas said; this building, owned by a member of the Kurtz family, was a garage. "It had a concrete-block side and a frame side, and for the concrete-block side we outfitted it with finishing materials and on the frame side we outfitted it with machinery so that we could make the furniture and accessories." Besides tables and chairs, the workmen would turn out beds, chests, candle stands, wooden coat hangers, and mirrors; hardware was reproduced in the mechanical maintenance shop headed by Carl Secchi. Thomas came to Pleasant Hill from Louisville, where he had worked on the restoration of Locust Grove, the home of George Rogers Clark, under the architect Walter Macomber, of Alexandria, Virginia, an old colleague of Jim Cogar's from Colonial Williamsburg, and with his own brother, Sam Thomas. A native of Chestnut Hill, Pennsylvania, a Philadelphia suburb, Jim Thomas at the age of fifteen "reluctantly" moved to Kentucky with his family, but by the next year his views had changed. He enjoyed his new classmates at Louisville Country Day, and when his father was transferred again, this time to Chicago, young Jim lasted for three days and then ran away from his new home, back to Louisville. After briefly attending the University of Louisville, Jim became "clerk of the works" at Locust Grove, where he and his brother also lived. Since very few persons had academic training in preservation in those days, Jim and Sam Thomas both learned the trade through on-the-job training.

On a visit to Louisville, Cogar met Thomas and, noting how he found the situation at Shaker Village reminiscent of the early days at Colonial Williamsburg, said he hoped that Thomas might join the project after finishing at Locust Grove. In an airport meeting in the summer of 1963 with Cogar and Earl Wallace, who was then commuting between Lexington and New York, Thomas was officially taken aboard; when he told the others that the arrangement was contingent on his work at Locust Grove being completed in 1964, Wallace commented that it was also contingent on Shakertown's having some money from the ARA loan. Fortunately, that turned out to be the case, and further, "I was fortunate," Thomas said, "to apprentice first under Walter Macomber and then under Jim Cogar, and I learned a tremendous amount from both." Cogar was "a marvelous person in every way. He had a magnetic personality, and he was a wonderful raconteur—an old-fashioned Kentucky storyteller. He had magnificent taste—an innate sense of style and taste."

Nora Belle Kurtz, whose family owned the country store and who presided at the Centre Family House during the May 31 restoration ceremony, was quite a story in herself. Betty Morris called her "the most delightful woman in the world," and to Jim Thomas she was "a wonderful person." He thought that, "growing up in the Depression, she had no advantages. She finished maybe the sixth or the eighth grade. But she was very smart and had a terrific work ethic." She began her association with the Pleasant Hill group as a volunteer, but when the organization began functioning she became perhaps the first local employee, presiding over the one room of crafts set up in the Centre Family House and directing tourists through the building, which for some time was, at best, only semirestored. She would go on to run, very successfully, the Pleasant Hill gift shop, and later to hold a vice presidency.

On the day before the ceremony, commenting on the progress of the project, Earl Wallace said in an eruption of wild optimism that the trustees hoped "to have the major part of the restoration done by the end of 1965." But the target date for opening the dining facilities and some of the guest rooms was even earlier, June 1965, just a year away. This represented an ambitious program, since no contracts would be let until late July or early August. As it turned out, quite a different schedule developed.

Having come from Colonial Williamsburg, where only one-sixth of the buildings stood as survivors from an earlier century, Jim Cogar brought a special perspective to his work in Mercer County. "The fascinating thing about Pleasant Hill," he once observed, "was that the buildings were still here and were in surprisingly good condition, considering the years they had been abandoned or used for other purposes. You could see the handwriting on the wall very plainly—it was a village that should be restored." Still, the degree of dilapidation and decay from which many of the buildings suffered meant that the restoration team faced daunting challenges, compounded by the less-than-ideal role forced on Cogar by the federal restrictions. The "excellence in everything" with which he credited the Shakers fitted exactly with his own drive for excellence, but with only limited authority over the workers on the job—and the number would grow to more than a hundred—he would have to draw on all his ingenuity to apply his dictum that "preservation is a science, not a haphazard affair."

Although the center of operations remained for some time in the office on Young Drive in Lexington, Cogar had earlier opened a Pleasant Hill office on the second floor of the Centre Family House at the very back of the building. "Cold in winter and hot in summer, it was primitive," he remembered. "People were still living there, including an elderly custodian on the floor below. We had a small shop in the basement of the East Family House, where we did most of the woodworking, making things needed in the repairs." Using scraps of wood found in attics and workrooms, craftsmen repaired windows, doors, and interior moldings with the initial aim of furbishing the Centre Family House enough to make it attractive to tourists. "Mrs. Kurtz, who ran the family's grocery, was a dynamo and was able to provide us with lunches as well as gasoline and 'most anything else we needed." Cogar was not a "sit-down-at-the-desk type man," Betty Morris said. "He ran things from walking around."

Washington Reed, who had begun helping with the loan application during the previous year, complemented Cogar with his preservation experience. A "delightful, gentle person," as Thomas remembered him, Reed and three other architects would spend two years making detailed drawings of the buildings, now reduced in the planning from twenty-seven to twenty, to be preserved and restored. Later, as inflationary pressures fueled by the Vietnam War built up, the number for the first phase of the restoration would be reduced to twelve and then to eight; the $2 million federal loan wouldn't stretch as far as had been hoped and expected.

Cogar visualized in detail the village as it had appeared in the chosen Shaker days. He wanted all "nonconforming" buildings removed and practical signs of the twentieth century must be invisible: all wires and pipes installed must be tunneled through the massive foundations of the buildings; all outside utility pipes and wires must be buried. The sewage-disposal plant would be placed out of sight. Cogar's contributions in working out the master plan for the adaptation of the buildings to functional uses were "of inestimable value in convincing government officials that Shakertown had the talent to make the most of the proceeds of the loan," Wallace said. "Not only that, but he was a stickler for authenticity to the extreme practicable in the circumstances, in which I supported him completely, as did the trustees"—even though this support often had a painful price: "At times we could have saved several hundred thousand dollars by not hiding in the walls and the grounds such installations as ducts, conduits, pipes, and wires for utilities and air-conditioning."

Overall, Cogar would carefully set the tone of the restoration. As a leading exponent of the idea of historic preservation as the capture of a moment in time, he represented the characteristic and best thought of his generation; thus at Pleasant Hill any features that came after about 1860 were removed from the scene. In later decades, many preservationists would move toward a different view, embracing the concept of showing change over time and thus tending to preserve features of buildings from different periods. This trend in preservationist fashion did not mean that Cogar had an incorrect or flawed philosophy; a restoration, like anything else, is, of course, a product of its era, and in their own moment in time the members of the Shakertown board, like Rockefeller at Williamsburg, seemed to favor the aesthetic appeal of seizing the single moment. They were, in a way, looking to the creation of a work of art.

Those who saw preservation from a more sociological or political viewpoint, and their number is said to have increased in the 1980s and 1990s, would incline to the evolutionary approach; this would certainly be true of self-styled radical historians like Michael Wallace, who was quoted on Williamsburg in chapter 4. This historian could, indeed, feel some justification in changes that have come to Williamsburg in later years, perhaps especially in the fence paint that is now allowed to flake and the horse droppings that now grace the streets. (This latter feature, however, does not guarantee greater psychological authenticity, since the impact of horse manure today is far different from its effect more than two centuries ago, when it was taken for granted as a feature of daily life.) With reference to the work at Shakertown, Jim Thomas observed that, in addition to buildings without a Shaker history that were removed, "there were some additions that were torn off or torn away back in the early sixties that would be retained today."

Speaking in the year 2000, Richard Moe, president of the National Trust for Historic Preservation, offered a definition with elements that could provide support for various views: "Historic preservation is the business of saving special places and the quality of life they support. It has to do with more than bricks and iron and columns and cobblestones. It has to do with the way individuals, families and communities come together in attractive and supportive environments."

In any case, Cogar's unwavering commitment to excellence and his ability to work effectively within the federal restrictions would prove to be money in the bank, as Earl Wallace would find when he called on potential donors. Pleasant Hill's status as a going concern, one respectable and even much admired, would earn him a different reception from the days when he had desperately sought funds for a project that, while it might sound worthwhile, existed partly on paper and mostly in talk and dreams. One donor, W. Rowell Chase, would very nicely say, "I first saw Shakertown in the early '30's, shortly after moving to Cincinnati from New England. At that time, it seemed to me to be an unusual town, and I could not understand why it was just sitting there deteriorating. I am glad that somebody else had more gumption than I to do something about it."

When Cogar retired at the beginning of 1974, Wallace summed up his contribution: "The restored village is as much the handiwork of Jim Cogar as the original was the genius of Micajah Burnett."

The next objective of Mr. Wallace and his associates is to buy nearly 2,000 acres of smiling Bluegrass farmland, entirely surrounding the village," commented the *Courier-Journal* in its inevitable editorial applauding the ARA loan. "The purchase would forever protect Shakertown from vulgar and unsuitable intrusions of the modern world. This is vital insurance for the future." This was precisely Jim Cogar's view as well. "I had seen in Williamsburg what could happen," Cogar said. "It becomes almost impossible to get the land you want—it's hard to get and very expensive."

Less than a month later, on February 2, Shakertown finally closed the long-mooted deal with the Gwinn brothers for their 1,921 acres of farmland, extending about a mile in all directions from the village. So efficiently had the Gwinns restored and managed the land during their tenure of more than twenty-five years that they now had one of the largest farming operations in the Blue Grass, with a tobacco yield of about 150,000 pounds and sometimes as many as a thousand head of cattle grazing the pastures. After some discussion, the Gwinns agreed to a price of $500 an acre, for a total of $963,000; the down payment would be $192,000. By now Shakertown, Inc., had a considerable history of making deals without any funds on hand, and the Gwinns could hardly have been surprised at Wallace's request for a six-month period in which to raise the down payment. The purchasers' lack of cash did not cast a shadow on the transfer ceremony, which took place on a bright, cold day in the field behind the West Family House Sisters' Shop, a vantage point that gave a panoramic view of Pleasant Hill's new acreage. Herbert Gwinn presented the deed to Earl Wallace, who was accompanied by an array of Shakertown supporters—Charlie Sturgill, Thomas Satterwhite (the treasurer of the Shakertown board), Bob Jewell, George Chinn, Willard Gabhart, Gene Royalty, Enos Swain, J. T. "Hop" Ingram, Jane Bird Hutton, and R. B. McClure, the lawyer who had endured some rough going with the Gwinns but had hung on to complete the deal; George Gwinn also witnessed the handover.

Taking full advantage of the enhancement of the project's status conferred by the EDA loan, Wallace began writing and telephoning possible donors, seeking a contribution of $12,500 each toward the down payment. As the results showed, Shakertown was indeed beginning to take on the aura of a going concern; this procedure not only brought in the needed money but launched relationships with several persons who would play important continuing roles in the Pleasant Hill story. Checks came in from Barry Bingham, Jere Beam, J. Graham Brown, George Norton Jr., and Elbert Sutcliffe, of Louisville; Harry Blum, a Chicago friend of Beam's; and Pansy (Mrs. Parker) Poe, a Mercer County landowner who lived in Thomasville, Georgia. With this success in hand, Wallace said, "I had the boldness to telephone Eli Lilly, whom I had never met, to ask him if Mr. Barry Bingham and I could come up to see him. After finding out that we were going to ask him for $12,500, he replied that there was no use for Barry and me to take such a long trip on a hot summer day. His check came the next day." This characteristically thoughtful response from the Indianapolis pharmaceutical tycoon represented the first step in a friendship that would prove notably fruitful for Shakertown.

Then a friend in Versailles, Kentucky, suggested that Wallace phone Mrs. W. Alton Jones in Maryland. Though she was another person Wallace had never met, he had been acquainted with her husband, the chairman of Cities Service Oil Company, who had been killed just three years earlier in the crash of an American Airlines flight in New York. Jones had been on his way to join former President Eisenhower on a fishing trip and had won a strange kind of renown when it came to light that he was carrying in his pockets some $20,000 in cash. What, everybody wondered, was the money for? (The usual conclusion, naturally, was that it was for political purposes.) Though Wallace was prepared to go to Maryland to meet with Mrs. Jones, she very agreeably saved him the trip and promptly sent in her $12,500 check; Pleasant Hill now had another important new friend. With the needed money in hand, Wallace could make the down payment and the coveted farm belt encircling Pleasant Hill now belonged to the corporation. The balance of the debt after the down payment was to be covered by twenty-year installment notes at 6 percent interest; this meant semiannual payments of $33,337.

To avoid any complications with the EDA through their new ownership of producing and profit-making farms, the Shakertown trustees decided to create a separate corporation, the Shakertown Land Company, to hold the property. By taking this action, Shakertown sidestepped a major problem: it avoided having to amend the financial projections contained in the application that had been approved, which might have caused delays and, worse, might have brought about a change of mind by the EDA on the ground that Shakertown was incurring a large debt that was not an essential part of the historic restoration. It therefore was necessary to keep the Gwinn farms out of the mortgage.

The fact that the restoration of the village was now assured would act to increase the value of the land, and Wallace and his associates had another value enhancer to point to: the state highway department had agreed to move Highway 68, rerouting it around the village, a step that, besides its other benefits, would create a mile of new frontage for the farm. By June 1965, rights-of-way had been obtained; the state would award the contract the following September. Moving the narrow, curving highway would indeed alleviate a dangerous situation as more and more visitors came, flocking in and out of buildings and crossing the road, and it would also do away with a distracting twentieth-century presence in the middle of the nineteenth-century village. (Cogar would be familiar with this kind of move from his experience at Williamsburg, where Rockefeller had banished the Chesapeake and Ohio Railroad from the town.) In addition, the move would create room for the construction of parking lots between the village and the highway. But beyond those points, Jim Cogar's master plan—the plan approved by the EDA—showed the highway removed from the village and replaced by the old macadam road; therefore, it had to be done. Otherwise, the EDA could tell the Louisville bankers that Wallace and his associates had not lived up to the promises they had made.

Wallace recalled that Cogar used to say, "'The only land I want is that which adjoins us,' and to that of course there was no end. We would get one piece and he'd immediately want to get the next one. We were able to get what finally came to our 2,250 acres of land. The protective area is one of the most important things we have. We have miles of protection for the village on every side." As Wallace once observed, "I had seen what happened to Old Sturbridge Village. It was honky-tonked to death." Commercial encroachment became so oppressive at Old Sturbridge, Wallace learned, that the board entertained the idea of buying land on a neighboring highway and, so to speak, giving the village a new front door and shutting up the old entrance.

In their determination to acquire all the surrounding land, Wallace and his fellow trustees went after the original Shaker ferry property. Stretching some thirty-eight hundred feet along the Kentucky River palisades, with two original buildings the Believers had used in their river trade, this tract represented the only land between the village and the river that had not been part of the Gwinn deal. Negotiations conducted by Charlie Sturgill produced a deal for $35,000, with a down payment of $8,000. This time the first payment came from Wallace himself, who advanced the money (and thus found himself in the unusual position of holding Shakertown's note).

Early in 1965 Shakertown, Inc., fulfilled a long-felt need by acquiring the only village building the corporation did not yet own, the Meeting House, which currently served as the home of the Shakertown Baptist Church. The trustees felt a special urgency in pursuing this property because of rumors that an oil company had its eye on it, a possibility that stirred up twentieth-century visions of glowing signs and gas pumps in the middle of the restored village. But the story had more to it than that. Possession of the Meeting House actually constituted the key to the restoration, because as long as the Baptists owned it the state highway could not be dug up, moved away, and replaced by an old stagecoach road.

In an unusual deal made in negotiations conducted largely by Houlihan and Cogar, the church drove a hard bargain. The deacons agreed to trade the building for 2½ acres of land down Highway 68 toward Harrodsburg, provided that Shakertown, Inc., would build a church and a parsonage on that land. Much later, in the continuing drive for property, the corporation would acquire other buildings, but this transaction gave it total possession of the village itself.

The new church and parsonage came with a price tag of $50,000; Nettie Jones gave the money as a personal gift, after Wallace and Cogar had paid her a visit at her home in Easton, Maryland. An outgoing woman, Mrs. Jones had not only become a friend of Pleasant Hill but, in a characteristic move by Wallace, had now been placed on the board of trustees. ("I am flattered that you see fit to ask me to help you," she wrote.) And the $50,000 was not the only yield of the visit—the W. Alton Jones Foundation gave $100,000 toward purchases of land. Later in the year, Mrs. Jones

shrewdly noted to Wallace: "I smile at the suggestion you make of completion of a project in Dec. '66. Jim will *never* finish, if I know him."

The prospect of still more money for buying land came in September
1965 from a promising new source. One day a group of officials from the
Sarah Mellon Scaife Foundation of Pittsburgh flew in to Blue Grass Field
in Lexington, having previously told Wallace in a phone call that they wanted
to take a look at Pleasant Hill and talk about the plans for restoring the
village. This development resulted from a conversation between a
Shakertown trustee, Julia Hallowell, and her friend Cordelia Scaife May, a
Mellon heiress. Having arranged a Kentucky-ham-and-biscuit picnic lunch
for the visitors, Wallace eagerly showed them around Pleasant Hill, though
he was a little perturbed that while "Jim Cogar had been able to clean up
part of the village," at this early stage of the restoration "several buildings
looked dilapidated to visitors."

When it came time to talk money, Wallace optimistically told one of
the bankers in the party that half a million dollars would do very nicely in
carrying the debt on the Gwinn farms. In response, the banker and a few
others spoke of giving perhaps $10,000 apiece; with impressive chutzpah,
Wallace rejected the offer as too small. The next day, back in Pittsburgh,
the banker phoned with a promise of $100,000. When Wallace, still look-
ing for the half-million, expressed his disappointment, the banker assured
him that when recipients made prudent use of donations, the foundation
usually gave further grants. This first contribution of $100,000, to be used
for land purchases "to further protect the Village and to add several Shaker
buildings to those already owned by the Pleasant Hill Corporation," proved
indeed to be the beginning of a beautiful friendship for Shakertown.

Shakertown, Inc., was now taking in considerable money, but it was
spending a great deal, too. By August 1965, 26 trustees had contributed
$442,000; 49 other donors had contributed $155,900; and 652 small con-
tributors had given $42,700, for a total of $640,600. But the chairman
issued a warning: "In order to preserve our objectives, we have had to assume substantial amounts of instalment financing which are so burden-
some that we should refinance as much of it as early as possible, and should
provide substantial funds, in addition, for numerous phases of the project
for which the proceeds of our long-term loan are not available." The fed-

eral loan would make a vital contribution, and it had brought credibility
with it, but strong fund-raising efforts would continue to be needed.

The last week in October saw one great success. Invited by Wallace to
visit Pleasant Hill, Mr. and Mrs. Eli Lilly came down from Indianapolis on
October 25 in their Rolls-Royce with their chauffeur at the wheel, meeting
Wallace in Louisville for lunch at the Pendennis Club. Afterward they trans-
shipped to Wallace's Oldsmobile sedan for the drive to Pleasant Hill, with
their chauffeur dutifully following them in their own car. The Lillys proved
to be likable and direct persons who avoided any ostentation and seemed
genuinely appreciative of small favors; Eli Lilly expressed his thanks for
"one of the most interesting days there ever has been." Something of an
antiquarian himself, Lilly wrote about early Indiana history and folklore,
and he edited the 1860s diary of Heinrich Schliemann, the discoverer of
Troy. As president of his company during the Depression, Lilly, unlike other
employers, did not lay off workers but instead kept them busy painting
walls, washing windows, and sweeping floors and sidewalks until the plant
could resume normal production. He even expanded the company's sales
force.

Before retiring for the night at the Beaumont Inn in Harrodsburg,
Lilly told Wallace that he and his wife would speak to the officials of the
Lilly Endowment about a $100,000 contribution to Shakertown (a sum
equal to perhaps $500,000 a generation later). When the couple came down
to breakfast the next morning, however, Lilly said things had changed,
giving Wallace an anxious moment until his guests told him that they had
decided, instead of bothering with the endowment and the fuss of a special
board meeting, just to give personal checks themselves, half of the amount
coming from each. This $100,000 represented the largest gift Shakertown
had received. Chuckling about the transaction in a later conversation with
his daughter, Wallace told her that the Lillys probably took the donation
"out of the grocery money."

W allace's earlier forecast of a substantially completed restoration by
the end of 1965 had proved overoptimistic—Washington Reed and
his associates could not produce all the finished drawings, which they created in the minute detail, until the middle of the year. At one point, in

February, Wallace reported to the board that work on the plans and specifications was "proceeding very slowly and many questions and problems
were developing." Then all plans and engineering specifications were offered for public bidding; Sullivan and Cozart of Louisville was chosen as
the general contractor, and in the end the project awarded twenty-one separate contracts, all the way from carpentry to plumbing and electricity. Bids
for overnight facilities for visitors and for construction of site utilities, for
instance, were taken only in April 1966, and on June 21 Wallace stabbed a
narrow shovel into the lawn next to the Centre Family House to turn the
first earth and begin the action.

In the meantime, tragedy had struck. Reed, whom everybody admired,
suffered a massive heart attack during the winter, but at first he seemed to
be recovering from it. On May 30, however, came the shocking news of his
death. "He was going to move here and actually supervise the restoration,"
Thomas said. "It was going to be the capstone of his career." Chuck Graves,
dean of the University of Kentucky College of Architecture and a Shakertown
trustee, agreed to take Reed's place as chief architect for the restoration.
Fortunately, Reed had done his work so thoroughly that the project could
be carried out just as he had visualized it. His assistant in his home office,
Wallace Taylor, came from Warrenton to serve as resident project manager—filling the post as required by the EDA regulations.

By now, though only the Centre Family House with its little museum
could be considered a standard tourist attraction, Pleasant Hill was drawing more than eighteen thousand visitors a year and showing signs of becoming a significant employer in Mercer County, with fifteen to twenty
persons serving as guides or turning out the reproductions of Shaker furniture and a half-dozen more operating the farm. Weavers across the state
were producing wool and burlap carpeting for the Paint Creek Weavers of
Paintsville, who had the contract for supplying rugs for the guest rooms;
curtains in authentic styles and colors would come from the Quicksand
Craft Center, another mountain enterprise hooked into this Blue Grass
restoration. Soon more guides and other workers of all kinds would be
required to meet the anticipated crowds of day visitors and overnight guests;
the latter were expected to number as many as a hundred.

But the shortage of money remained a chronic problem. In a brilliant bit of co-opting, Wallace had persuaded Henry Offutt to join the board, and in June 1966 the Louisville banker became chairman of the finance committee. This was just in time for the two of them to propose to the Gwinn brothers that Shakertown not pay its next installment on the land purchase, due on July 1, but simply hand over the interest portion on this and future installments for the next five years, while giving 6 percent notes for the principal due during this time. This move, Wallace noted succinctly, would "reduce the annual burden of making cash payments."

At the same time, the board voted to authorize Wallace to buy still more land, this time some 120 acres down the hill on Shawnee Run (later called Shaker Creek), the site of the original settlement of the Shakers, which had contained the gristmill, sawmill, and linseed oil mill, and part of the orchards. This area was once crossed by a covered bridge and later by a bridge still called the Kissing Bridge. The money for this acquisition would come from the lady who had become one of Pleasant Hill's best friends, Nettie Jones. "I can remember him calling her when he had to have money," Betty Morris said. "He would say, 'Now, Nettie, we need this or that,' and she would come through."

Only one more land acquisition remained—for the time being. Not much more than a quarter of a mile from Shakertown, on the road leading to Danville through Burgin, stood the Shakertown School on a tract of about three acres. As school consolidation came to Mercer County, the board of education announced that this building would be put up for sale at a public auction. Here was the kind of situation Jim Cogar feared: a piece of property like this could pass into the hands of somebody who would set up a commercial operation of some kind right in Pleasant Hill's front yard and destroy or at least impair the carefully crafted illusion of a trip back in time.

Shortly before the auction, Wallace and his colleagues learned that an entrepreneur from Indiana intended to buy the school property and establish a trailer park with a fast-food stand to serve all the hundreds of fishermen who regularly passed by bound for Herrington Lake a few miles beyond. A local Mercer County contractor turned out to have similar plans, and as the sale opened the two competitors quickly ran the price up to $16,000, which was about what buyers had paid for other county schools. But, not stopping there, the bidding moved on, breaking $20,000. Despite that, Wallace said, "we felt that Shakertown must have the property for protection, so I began to bid, under Mr. Herbert Gwinn's guidance, until it was awarded to Shakertown at $25,000."

Now arose a familiar situation: Shakertown did not have the $25,000. "We paid 10 percent down," Wallace said, "and took a chance on raising the balance due in thirty days." To lessen the odds on this gamble, Wallace turned to Cordelia Scaife May of Pittsburgh, who had already given highly tangible proof of her interest in the conservation of the land surrounding Pleasant Hill. Mrs. May did not disappoint Wallace, promptly providing the needed balance; she even sent her "money manager" to Kentucky to counsel Wallace and his associates. Shakertown, Inc., now possessed more than half of the 4,369 acres owned by the Shakers at the height of their prosperity.

As the restoration progressed through 1966 and into 1967, friends of Shakertown could find considerable satisfaction in the knowledge that the project was reaping the benefits of having a hard-driving financier to keep it going and an aesthetic perfectionist to make it appealing to the press and the public. But the third side of the triangle remained open until one January day in 1967, when Earl Wallace and Betty Morris drove to Louisville for a meeting at the downtown Pendennis Club with a lady named Elizabeth Cromwell Kremer.

A native of Cynthiana, Kentucky, Mrs. Kremer (who was Mrs. Morris's aunt and thus was one of Bob Jewell's numerous cousins) could claim as much specialized standing in her field as Wallace could in his. After receiving her degree in home economics from the University of Kentucky, she had gone to New York, where she had become a food manager for the Schrafft's restaurant chain and then for another chain called Ship Grill. Returning to the Ohio Valley, she had worked in the restaurant business in Cincinnati and then had opened the French Village restaurant, part of the Canary Cottage chain, in the Heyburn building in downtown Louisville, where she acquired a strong local following. Something of a pioneering woman as a restaurant executive, she then went back to Cincinnati to open and manage the Canary Cottage there, and also got married. Her husband,

Harold Kremer, was a construction engineer who was frequently trans-
ferred, and Mrs. Kremer soon retired from business, devoting much of her
time to rearing her two daughters; by 1967, in fact, she had been out of the
restaurant business for twenty-six years.

But everybody, including her old school friend Jim Cogar, remembered her fame as a food expert. Though Pleasant Hill was not yet ready for
dining rooms, Wallace, looking ahead, had talked with and been turned
down by two companies that operated historic inns in New England and
Virginia. One explained that the rural location of Pleasant Hill and the
limited space in the Trustees' House would work together to keep the operation from turning a profit. This judgment came as particularly dis-
turbing news to Wallace because his projections for the EDA had presented
the dining rooms and guest rooms as moneymakers. Inspired by favorable
mention of Elizabeth Kremer on all sides and also, perhaps, by the regional
fame of Cynthiana as an incubator of good cooks, Wallace in early 1966
sent out a feeler to her, but she, too, turned him down.

Now, as work proceeded on the buildings and the grounds at Pleasant
Hill, people by the hundreds came to look at what was happening. Mrs. Kremer's
husband had died in November 1966, and the mission that sent Wallace
and Betty Morris to Louisville was to try to recruit her to come to Shakertown
and establish and operate a sandwich shop to serve the sightseers.
She did not immediately accept this proposition—she was sixty-five now
and had not worked in business since 1941. She was interested but doubtful; as Betty Morris said, "The whole restaurant business had changed so
much. When she was running things, people were dying to work. And
there was no frozen food, and all that." But since the idea of filling her time
with this new project had its appeal, too, Mrs. Kremer decided to ask her
daughters "if they thought she could do it at such an old age." They responded with enthusiasm, telling her that "it would be a marvelous new
life" for her and that she had no reason to stay in Louisville. And Wallace as
always had his own brand of persuasion.

Mrs. Kremer soon had a snack-and-sandwich operation up and running in the Old Stone Shop, which had served as the home and office of
Dr. W. F. Pennebaker, the last Shaker physician and the man who had
made the arrangement with George Bohon, the Harrodsburg businessman,

whereby the Shakers deeded their land in exchange for Bohon's agreement to care for them until their deaths. Pennebaker proved to be the next to last of the Shakers, being survived only by Mary Settles. This Shaker history played a part in luring Mrs. Kremer to Pleasant Hill, since she had known Sister Mary. "I really have a great respect and admiration for the Shakers," Mrs. Kremer once said, "and enjoy trying to bring a little of what they had here—integrity and hospitality."

Although a tiny, seemingly frail woman, just five feet tall, Mrs. Kremer proved to have an abundance of energy. Having held managerial positions during the Depression, as Betty Morris noted, she expected an employee to put in a good day's work; "she was hard-driving but fair," as Jim Thomas put it. Mrs. Kremer soon found herself helping to design and equip the kitchen and dining rooms in the Trustees' House. She had promised to come for two months but agreed stay on at Pleasant Hill as director of food service, as Wallace had no doubt hoped and expected.

The triangle was now complete, and it had three perfectionist sides. By the end of 1967 the first stage of the restoration had been completed—the buildings were finished and they had been furnished in proper Shaker style. Although not all of the *t*'s were crossed and *i*'s dotted, the government inspectors had approved the work and all the contractors and suppliers had been paid. With Phase One finished, Wallace and the other trustees now looked to launching Phase Two, this time not under strict government controls but with money from private sources.

But first would come the opening of the restored Pleasant Hill to the general public. Having decided to wait until spring, the board planned a shakedown operation for early April, to try the dining room and test the beds; both food and lodging passed this examination. Afterward, one delighted member wrote Cogar, "This dream could *never* have come true without you at the helm, Jim—*everyone* knows this." Then, on April 15, in a relatively low-key event, the Shaker Village at Pleasant Hill officially opened its doors to all comers. Tourists could now go through six buildings, spend the night in any of fifty-two guest rooms, all furnished with reproduction—and some original—Shaker pieces, and eat in the dining rooms in the Trustees' House.

Elizabeth Kremer could now move on from sandwiches to full-scale menus. "I can remember," said her daughter Evalina Settles, "that she got everything she could read on the Shakers, as far as the food went, and that's where they got the Shaker lemon pie that became so famous. They were able to pull in women who knew how to cook—farm wives and others who were good basic cooks and wanted jobs. I can't tell you how many books she got her hands on that told you what types of food the Shakers had. She wanted to keep it simple, which is what the Shakers did."

These simple meals, which would quickly win regional and even wider renown, would feature, along with cornerstones like roast beef, pork tenderloin, and chicken, such favorites as corncakes, stuffed peppers, tomato celery soup, and eggplant, and pies—chess as well as Shaker lemon—that would bring in customers all by themselves. According to one of her daughters, Mrs. Kremer had one standard bit of advice about cooking: "Always taste your food. If it suits you, then it will please your guests." As Jim Thomas put it, "She established the standard for excellence here." She would serve for twenty-one years and would produce two cookbooks, *We Make You Kindly Welcome* and *Welcome Back to Pleasant Hill*, which would enjoy perpetual popularity.

The facilities at Pleasant Hill would quickly win favorable comment on all sides, but no judgment seemed more sound than that of Nettie Jones, who came from Maryland for the trustees' shakedown overnighter and, back home, wrote Cogar that she was "thrilled" over the visit. "I think things ran *very* smoothly for a 'trial run,'" she said. "And all the guests were really home folks celebrating a *fantastic* accomplishment in an unbelievably short time."

What Mrs. Jones did not know was that, at the time, the bank balance of Shakertown, Inc., amounted to no more than $500.

CHAPTER X

The Deal—II

❦

A few days after the official opening of Shakertown, Earl Wallace received a memo from the maintenance department. Headed, portentously, PRIORITIES, this document contained a list of tasks to be performed, "broken down into categories and arranged in the order of their importance."

LANDSCAPING
1. Distribute and lay sod when cut from garden plots.
2. Clean up, grade and seed around north end of East Family House.

CARPENTRY
1. Complete installation of blinds on Trustees' Office.
1. Prepare 1st floor of Farm Deacon's Shop for snack bar.
2. Trash Yard back of Trustees' Office.
2. Linen Room shelving.
3. Complete exterior deck—East Family House.
4. Post and rail fence—Farm Deacon's Shop, east to drive past E. Family Sisters' Shop.

PAINTING
1. Complete North Porch—East Family House.
2. Snack Bar—Farm Deacon's Shop.
2. Whitewash Linen Room.

2. Louver over doors—East side Trustees' Office.
3. Fences and trash yard.

Such operational details were primarily the concern of Jim Cogar and Jim Thomas, while Wallace chiefly dwelt in the realm of high finance (almost all of it relating to Shakertown, since he had ended his connection with Dillon Read in 1967). The chairman, however, also concerned himself with all aspects of the operation having to do with expenditures, from the largest to the most minute—the best buys in water coolers, the best deals in detergents. At this time he was pushing the Department of Highways to provide numerous signs on all the roads leading to Pleasant Hill, an effort that elicited from the director of the Division of Traffic an agreement to have five signs put up on Highways 68 and 33 and the possibly weary observation that, even though Wallace had asked for many more, "we do believe that the guidance needs of strange motorists seeking Shakertown will be adequately served." During these same days, Thomas was also dealing with the Progress Paint Manufacturing Company, which was producing a line of "Shakertown paints"—in Trustees' Office Brown, East Family Blue, Centre Family Blue, West Family Blue, Brethren's Shop Red, and, for exteriors, Pleasant Hill Shutter Green and Pleasant Hill Yellow—for general sale and for the Pleasant Hill gift shop; Shakertown, Inc., would receive a 5 percent royalty on the distributors' price.

The government loan had saved the Pleasant Hill project, as everyone knew, making possible the Phase One restoration; but "beyond that," Wallace said, "it was just a continual grind." Fortunately, "we were able to interest some people that had a certain spirit that I'd never come into contact with before. You don't work for the Standard Oil Company and Wall Street firms and meet anybody except those who are chasing the almighty dollar." With Shakertown, however, he had come to know people "that had a different slant on life" from what he had known.

Now that he had something to show such potential donors, his method of approaching them involved inviting them to Pleasant Hill to see for themselves the quality of the craftsmanship and the taste shown in the appointments and furnishings. At the executive committee meeting of May 12, Wallace reported that some of these donors had given funds to carry out Phase Two restoration of four buildings—the Water House, the West Family Sisters' Shop, the Meeting House, and the West Family Wash House. The Water House had a special claim to fame as the reputed first water-works west of the Allegheny Mountains, but the building now seemed to be leaning toward collapse. As Wallace was walking by this wreck one day with one of his philanthropic friends, Pansy Poe, she had turned to him, saying, "I'm tired of looking at it, so you go ahead and have Mr. Cogar restore it before it falls down, and I'll give you the money."

Work on the Meeting House and the West Family Wash House, Wallace told the trustees, could begin as soon as the needed scaffolding arrived; meanwhile, the plans for heating, air-conditioning, and plumbing would have to be worked out. Now free of the constraints of the Davis-Bacon Act, the chairman recommended that Cogar assign to Taylor a force of carpenters, helpers, and laborers who would work exclusively on this program and that Shakertown make local contracts for the mechanical and electrical installations. Pointing out that the organization had "most of the roofing on hand and certain air handling equipment," he expressed his intention to arrange with suppliers more liberal discounts on materials. (Cogar did succeed in creating a cost-cutting team from workers already on the pay-roll, men who were local and thus nonunion—two carpenters and two helpers, and a stonemason and helper; electrical work was carried out by the maintenance staff with the help of a local electrician and plumber. "We took the crew that I had trained to be furniture makers," Thomas said, "and made them millworkers and carpenters.")

Wallace then led the committee through a discussion of operating problems that had already arisen. Parking, the plague of almost every enterprise that caters to the public, seemed to rank Number One, particularly with guests who came for lunch and found themselves required to walk some three hundred yards from the parking lot to the inn, since Cogar wanted to keep cars off the village street. (The possibility of parking on this street would disappear within three months. With Highway 68 now bypassing Shakertown, the asphalt surface of the street would be torn up and replaced with dirt and gravel, with turf lining both sides, thus bringing it back to its nineteenth-century look as a stagecoach road, as shown in Lewis Collins's famous *Historical Sketches of Kentucky*, published in 1847.) Cogar had proposed a compromise plan whereby drivers would drop off their passengers at the inn and then return their cars to the parking lot. Wallace wished to move carefully in this realm in order to avoid creating word-of-mouth complaints and loss of luncheon business. "The question is," he said, "should we risk it or should we tolerate cars on the street until we can build a parking lot for Inn guests?"

Much attention went to promotion and advertising. Revenue from guest rooms was suffering because Wallace and others felt that these accommodations should not be advertised until "bugs" could be eliminated in the heating and air-conditioning controls, in which piping had been improperly installed. These problems seemed likely to linger until the contractor, who was proving to be uncooperative, could be induced to correct the mistakes. The shortage of overnight guests, in turn, was affecting sales of dinner and breakfast. "Only the most complimentary response has been heard of the quality of the food," Wallace said, with the result that the luncheon business had surpassed all expectations, with many customers returning accompanied by members of their various clubs and groups. Wallace also reported a particular piece of good promotional news: the August issue of *Woman's Day*, a magazine with a very large circulation, would carry a Shakertown story by Michael Frome, a leading travel writer of the time. The village had already received fine notices in a number of newspapers, including, of course, the faithful *Courier-Journal*.

After discussing a number of other matters, Wallace presented a new organizational chart, the most important aspect of which was the delineation of the functional responsibilities of Jim Cogar and Betty Morris. Subject to the approval of the executive committee, Cogar, the executive director (in 1969 he would assume the title of president), would have charge of village operations and restoration. Mrs. Morris, meanwhile, would function in a double role: she would supervise rooms, housekeeping, reservations, and the staffing of the front desk, reporting to Cogar, and as assistant secretary and assistant treasurer, she would have charge of financial controls and reports and all business-office personnel and functions, reporting in this role to the chairman and the executive committee. In the former role, Mrs. Morris functioned much like the manager of a hotel, and she took a serious view of her responsibilities, being known for never putting a newly decorated and furnished room into service until she had slept in it herself. Once, she recalled, when she and her husband spent the night in one of the smaller rooms in the West Family House, they discovered that the floor had such a pronounced slope that the head of the bed was lower than the foot. The problem was solved with blocks.

The new organizational chart listed Jim Thomas as staff assistant for operations, but in September he received the new title of curator, with responsibility for interpretation and expansion of the exhibits, improvements on the village grounds, and management of the craft sales shop. As he would discover, getting the buildings into full service was the first step; after that, somebody would have to administer the restoration, and much of that administration fell to him as curator: "We had to develop programs and uses for these buildings."

In spite of the varied problems associated with launching the full-fledged operation, Pleasant Hill in reality had gotten off to a solid start. By August a reporter could note that since early May the dining rooms had attracted about three hundred customers a day, two or three times as many as had been expected, with 250 once being served at lunch "on a Tuesday, of all days." The management now urged guests to make reservations for all meals on weekends and for lunch every day, and this success led to the decision to keep Pleasant Hill open all winter. Several reasons lay behind this popularity, including Shakertown's proximity to Louisville and, even more, to Lexington, and the high good taste that characterized the restoration. "Finally," noted the reporter, sounding like an echo of his Cincinnati counterpart who had dined at Pleasant Hill more than a century earlier, "the meals are delicious," with all the vegetables served being grown in gardens adjacent to the inn. This comment went straight to the point, since one of Mrs. Kremer's concerns on reentering the restaurant world had been the great increase in the use of packaged foods. That was most emphatically not her style, even though she had to train some of the employees in the use of fresh vegetables.

Another writer spoke highly of the service, with food being brought by "demure-looking" waitresses in yellow or brown fine-check ankle-length dresses, with white aprons and kerchiefs and Shaker caps made of net. Like the plan to furnish the rooms in Shaker style to give guests something of the atmosphere in which the builders of the village had lived, the idea of dressing waitresses, busboys, and other employees in costumes was the brainchild of Jim Cogar. Seeing all these people moving around in their Shaker uniforms would, he believed, constantly remind the visiting public of the Shaker story. At dinnertime the dining rooms and the halls were lighted entirely by candles, and each table bore a card, reproduced from a handwritten original: "We make you kindly welcome to Pleasant Hill." But one of the writers also commented on how much space was available for those who wanted to spend the night, though he proffered an analysis far simpler than any conclusions reached by management: it proved that "more people like to eat than sleep."

Aside from praises in the press, Shakertown built goodwill by its responsiveness to requests of all kinds. A very young man from Maysville, for instance, wrote to say that on a recent family visit his father had bought one of the glasses used in the "restrorount" but that "the other day, it broke and he was very mad." Implicitly, at least, acknowledging some culpability in this mysterious mishap, the boy enclosed a dollar with the request that Shakertown send him the replacement glass before Christmas. The staff readily complied, with somebody making a marginal notation, before filing the letter, that the postage came to 65 cents.

By the end of 1968, Shakertown had played host to some 50,000 guests, and the management looked forward to receiving perhaps 90,000 in the coming year and ultimately 150,000, a total that had figured in the early forecasts of advisers from Williamsburg. Organizations of all kinds also were beginning to hold meetings at Pleasant Hill. In February 1969, Wallace listed a number of forthcoming events—the Kentucky League of Sportsmen in that same month; in March, area businessmen, officers of the Civil War Round Table, and travel editors; in April, editors of metropolitan newspapers and, perhaps, judges of the Court of Appeals; and in May wives of Republican governors, whose husbands would be holding their national meeting in Lexington. These occasions had their high points, as occurred when the governors' ladies came to Pleasant Hill. As Jim Cogar squired the first ladies around the grounds, he described certain key beliefs held by the Shakers, and, turning to Nancy Reagan, wife of the governor of California, asked whether she might be converted. "To being a Kentuckian?" she asked.

"No," he replied, "a Shaker." "No," responded Mrs. Reagan, "I don't like those ground rules."

Improvements would continue to be made and more buildings to be restored under Phase Two plans—the West Family House, the Old Ministry's Shop, the Tanyard House, the Farm Deacon's Shop, the Post Office (which years before had been moved several hundred feet from its original site and used as a tenant house, and now would be returned to its original foundation near the Trustees' House and turned into a second craft shop—with the Carpenters' Shop remaining the principal craft store), the East Family Wash House, the Cooper's Shop, and the Centre Family House. The last-named building, the large stone structure that sat imposingly in the middle of the village, had been reasonably well restored inside but needed a thorough makeover on the outside. The windows were missing their green shutters, the roof balustrade was gone, the roof leaked, the bell tower was rotting away, and the cellar had been stripped down to the clay.

During the next few years, the chief fund-raiser and his colleagues would have to find money to carry out all of these purposes; the Phase Two work would continue until 1974. Meanwhile, in 1970 the Society of American Travel Writers gave Pleasant Hill its imprimatur with one of its "Connie" awards, and *Holiday* magazine presented its "Holiday Award for a Beautiful America," calling the village "a museum of the highest quality which preserves, for the citizens of Kentucky and for the nation, a portion of our pasts." In 1971 the National Register of Historic Places added Shakertown to its listing with this enthusiastic and genuinely insightful citation: "The large number and type of original Shaker buildings at Pleasant Hill and the fact that they still exist in their virtually unaltered rural setting make Shakertown at Pleasant Hill an architectural and spiritual experience unsurpassed in the United States." In September 1972, Secretary of the Interior Rogers C. B. Morton presented a certificate and plaque declaring Shakertown at Pleasant Hill a National Historic Landmark. Wallace had sought the help of Morton's older brother, Senator Thruston B. Morton of Louisville, in getting the secretary to come from Washington to make the presentation in person; the trustees held a "private" luncheon for the secretary, Governor Wendell Ford, and members of the Kentucky Heritage Commission.

By April 1972, just four years after its opening, Pleasant Hill had achieved some remarkable results. It had reached the goal of 150,000 visitors a year (614,000 people had come between April 1968 and April 1972, and 330,000 of them had eaten at least one meal; 36,000 had spent the night, and 250,000 had visited the exhibits that told the Shaker story). The figures demonstrated the economic impact of Pleasant Hill on the area: the project had paid out $1.4 million to its employees, it had purchased $321,000 worth of goods and supplies in Mercer and neighboring Boyle counties and $297,000 worth in Lexington, and it had bought $96,000 worth of items from Appalachian craftspersons for sale in the gift shops. Most striking, perhaps, it had clearly justified the projections contained in the original application to the Area Redevelopment Administration by becoming the second-largest taxpayer in Mercer County. Three years later, despite the general tightening of auto travel imposed by the gasoline shortages of 1974–1975, Shakertown produced further impressive figures: the village fed 130,000 people and drew 26,000 overnight guests; the payroll for the year amounted to $600,000.

Always concerned with increasing net income, Wallace, though pleased about the play Pleasant Hill received in national magazines and metropolitan newspapers, complained that the writers of these articles concentrated on the food and the accommodations and seldom made "any reference to the exhibits or what visitors might see in the buildings." Examining the stories with a close eye, he cited an example from *Southern Living*, "9 column inches with pictures, with only ¾ths of an inch on the exhibits." Similarly, a newspaper travel section gave Pleasant Hill 45 column inches and pictures with only "a 1¼ inch reference to the exhibits." What particularly frustrated Wallace was the failure of a promotional campaign, which he had induced Cordelia Scaife May to finance to the tune of $25,000 a year for two years, to rectify this situation. Although the promotional director, a young woman named Marcia Axtmann, waged a vigorous campaign—with news releases, television and radio tapes, feature stories, and promotional kits and folders—ticket sales to the exhibits stayed flat; writers stubbornly stuck to praising the food and the rooms and the general atmosphere. (A capable person highly esteemed by Wallace, Miss Axtmann left Shakertown to take a job with the National Trust in Washington, a

move that upset the chairman, who believed that she had been hijacked by
the Trust; most likely, however, Miss Axtmann, a native of Zanesville, Ohio,
had decided that she had put in enough time in small towns and wanted to
move to a city. Carl Humelsine, president of the Trust and of Colonial
Williamsburg, phoned Jim Thomas to ask him to assure Wallace that Miss
Axtmann had applied for the job and had not been stolen away.)

Speaking with a writer from the *Ford Times* (the most renowned of
automobile company magazines, with a circulation of 2 million), Wallace
"noted her interest primarily in the village as a place to spend the night and
enjoy good food. She mentioned the quality of the merchandise in the
craft shops but made a remark that museums turn her off." What could
you do with somebody like that?

As a gratifying by-product of everybody's labors, the work at Pleasant
Hill exerted a consciousness-raising effect across the state of Kentucky.
Thousands of people saw what was happening, and "as restoration progressed," Wallace said, "many began to think of restoring historic buildings
in their own community. We know this because we were asked by many
groups for advice on how to proceed with their local projects. There is
every indication that Pleasant Hill has been a major factor in arousing local
interest that has now emerged as a burgeoning movement of historic preservation in Kentucky."

Despite all of the praise and all of the achievements, Shakertown proved
a continuingly expensive operation to maintain. In the fall of 1969,
with outgo exceeding income—and capital funds unavailable for operational use because they were dedicated to restoration—it became clear that
the project would not have enough cash on hand to meet the December
payroll, and for the succeeding months the outlook seemed even worse.
Unless Wallace or somebody else could tap a donor for a quick transfusion,
it seemed, the trustees might actually have to close the village. For help in
this emergency, Wallace, feeling that by now the Shakertown trustees had
been milked almost dry, ruled these friends out and turned instead to the
couple who belonged to the top four or five of Pleasant Hill's most faithful
admirers, the Lillys, who ever since their first visit had driven down for a
stay every April and October. Talking with Eli Lilly, Wallace asked him "if

he could get us through the winter." Lilly did not hesitate; he said that "he would arrange to get us through two winters, which he did"—by means, perhaps, of another dip into the family's grocery money, this one amounting to $200,000.

As for the government loan, it had achieved its purpose, but it had not then quietly faded into history. Instead, it remained a daily nagging presence, demanding the accumulation of funds for the regular interest payments; Wallace's drive to increase ticket sales was fueled by the need to get net income to the level that would meet these payments. For the first two years after opening—1968 and 1969—Shakertown paid the interest mostly out of small, unrestricted contributions. But in February 1969 Wallace was already asking the trustees to approve a request to the EDA to add that year's interest payment to the loan and also to defer the interest to November 1970 and put off for two years the date when payments of principal would have to begin. He would justify the request by pointing out that the village had opened a year later than planned, that the cost of materials had risen greatly because of inflation during the period of the restoration, and that the corporation needed a year's grace in order to begin accumulating funds.

What happened was that in the next two years, without an accumulation of cash and with the sizable capital funds not available, Shakertown, Inc., could make no payment, and it technically went into default in November 1970. "With a dim prospect of meeting the payments in the next two years," Wallace said with commendable understatement, "I could see four years in default, probably enough to embarrass our relations with the EDA officials." In fact, the financial situation he had foreseen and probably had expected at the time of making the original application had now arrived. Telling the board that he expected a lean winter (and taking time to recommend that Jim Thomas and Betty Morris be elected vice presidents), he went off to Washington carrying an ingeniously simple if audacious proposal: the EDA should agree to amend the original contract, waiving loan payments for the next four years; Wallace wanted to amend the old agreement rather than execute a new one in order to preserve the $3^5/8$ percent interest; otherwise the rate would now have become 6 percent.

As EDA officials chewed over the proposition, Wallace made return trips to Washington to push the plan along. Early in the game, shrewdly, he asked Governor Louie B. Nunn to accompany him on one visit, on the presumption that, as Kentucky's first Republican governor since the mid-1940s, Nunn could exert a benign influence on officials of the Nixon administration, which had come to office the preceding year. Wallace's analysis proved to be quite correct—"he was better than a new hand," Nunn said in admiring recollection. Having previously developed a strong relationship with Nixon, Nunn made an advance call to the White House and went on to make quick and effective use of the administration's network.

"When Nixon was president," Nunn explained, "they had in every department a political person who, if the White House wanted something to be done, would get the message from the administration. I had the names and telephone numbers of those people in every department. If I wanted something done, I could call [John] Ehrlichman or [Bob] Haldeman and ask them to please contact their man in the department and see what they could do to help us. There was a little politics involved in it, and, you know, some people frown on that. But we saved Shakertown, let's put it that way—however it was done—and absolutely nothing wrong occurred. They had the money there, and they were trying to help people who were trying to help themselves." At the offices of the EDA, the governor made a most emphatic affirmation of the significance of Pleasant Hill and, as Wallace put it, "urged the EDA officials to assist the organization in every way possible."

Still, it was only after a year and a half of negotiations that the EDA agreed to amendments to the contract, but when these changes came they were sweeping. The unpaid interest for the years from 1970 through 1973, totaling $290,000, was rolled together in a new note at $3^5/8$ percent and then consolidated with the old note, giving a new total for the loan of $2,290,000. Payments—*of interest only*—would begin in 1974 and continue through 1979; each of these would be for $83,012. Payments of principal and interest together would not begin until 1980, and they would continue for thirty-five years, until 2014. Wallace was "a great analyzer," said one associate; "he could analyze situations and just tear them apart," and now he had succeeded in producing an agreement in which the debt was increased, the time to pay was extended, the pre–Vietnam War interest rate was retained, and nothing at all had to be paid for four years. Louie Nunn remained impressed that Wallace came away with more money than had been awarded in the original loan.

In staging this remarkable coup, Wallace had fully confirmed his view of the difference between the government and an array of private investors as the creditor. While the EDA officials had dealt very carefully with the situation—"and there was a little politics involved," as Nunn said—the market would have taken a much different course. "If bonds had been issued against this project, as the government originally intended, and sold to private investors," Wallace observed, "it would have been impossible to have renegotiated this loan with all the bondholders [even presuming that any would have been willing to do it], any one of whom could have foreclosed the mortgage after the first default in 1970."

Even after making this highly advantageous deal, Wallace saw more clouds on Pleasant Hill's fiscal horizon. From 1974 through 1979, Shakertown, Inc., would have to produce a total of $498,072 in interest payments; but as inflation and new legislation pushed up the cost of operating the village from year to year—utility bills, social security contributions, unemployment taxes, postage, and wages were all going up—it hardly seemed likely that this sum could come out of profits from village operations. This time Wallace proposed that the board establish an endowment fund, with a target of $1 million; the income would be dedicated to the annual payments on the loan. The board agreed, and within less than three years the fund had taken in about $800,000. The income, together with profits from village operations, amounted to enough to meet the payments that began in 1974.

But Wallace saw this improvement as only temporary, as the so-called stagflation of the Carter administration years and two of the most brutal winters of the twentieth century took their toll on Pleasant Hill. In 1977, for the first time since 1970, the village operated at a loss. In mid-March 1978, the funds built up from village operations had declined to $35,000, a sum in itself little more than enough to meet the next two-week payroll. Happily, this situation did not affect the work of restoration, because in 1975 the ever dependable Lilly Endowment had agreed to supply $360,000 to carry out the entire Phase Three program over the three years to 1978, beginning with the North Lot Dwelling, the West Family Dwelling, and an archaeological survey of the mill area on Shaker Creek. Lilly grants never came with restrictions, which meant that the money could be used not only for restoring major buildings but also for unglamorous details such as improving service roads and parking lots. Jim Cogar retired as president at the beginning of 1974, being succeeded by Jim Thomas, who had now held his curatorial post for six years and had been executive vice president since 1971; Betty Morris became executive vice president and treasurer. From now on, Thomas would preside over Phase Three and all subsequent restoration work.

Ultimately, Mr. and Mrs. Lilly personally, together with the Lilly Endowment, proved to be the largest donors to Shakertown. An uncounted number of these dollars flowed into Pleasant Hill because of the extraordinary level Wallace's persistence could reach. One Monday morning in 1972 the chairman had chattily informed Betty Morris that he had seen the Lillys during the weekend. "Oh," she said, never surprised at anything Wallace did, "you went to Indianapolis?" No, that wasn't the case, Wallace said. He had gone up to the Lillys' weekend and summer retreat, in far northeastern Indiana on Lake Wawasee. After driving a long stretch down an obscure country road, he had found the Lillys' cottage; he was just passing by, he told them, and thought it would be nice to drop in for a few minutes. Mrs. Morris had a good laugh at the story, but Wallace later asserted that he never mentioned Shakertown's need for more money. Regardless of that, his surprised hosts seemed to get the message.

Though business in the 1980s would turn out to be better than the prospect seemed from the vantage point of the late 1970s, crisis appeared to have become the permanent characteristic of Pleasant Hill's fiscal operations. But those who had admired Wallace's handling of the original loan application and had been dazzled by his renegotiation of the agreement would now have the opportunity to see what a master dealmeister could really do when pressed. Looking ahead toward 2014, Wallace saw Shakertown, Inc., having to make thirty-five loan payments, at $116,515 each, for a total of more than $4 million; endowment income might supply about $2.2 million of that, leaving a balance to be made up from village net income of about $1.8 million. The late 1970s did not produce much optimism in economic observers anywhere, and Wallace's outlook no doubt took some of its tone from the prevailing gloom. But beyond that, he saw that Pleasant Hill could build up the income balance it needed only by raising prices beyond those the public was willing to pay. (Just to take one factor among many affecting costs, congressional action on Social Security and the minimum wage meant bumps of 65 percent and 45 percent, respectively, resulting in more than double-digit percentage increases in payrolls.)

In Wallace's view, the path to transforming the situation did not lead through further postponements of payments or further extensions to the life of the loan. Clearly, the answer lay in getting rid of the debt entirely! A wonderfully desirable goal, no doubt, but how could it be accomplished? In March 1978, meeting with EDA officials in Washington, Wallace proposed, of all things, that the EDA sell the note to Shakertown, Inc. What he had in mind was that the sale be made at the current market value of the note, which he put at no more than $750,000, because of the $3^5/8$ percent interest rate and long maturity. No one recorded his facial expression as he pointed out to the officials that a high discount factor was obviously necessary to equate the yield with that produced by the rates of 10 percent and more currently prevailing in the money markets, and presumably he did not further point out to his EDA friends that it was his earlier renegotiation that had preserved the old $3^5/8$ percent rate so advantageous for Shakertown.

Without the burden of the annual payments of $116,515 that would begin in 1980 and go on until 2014, Wallace said—making the kind of argument that might come from the finance minister of a Third World country dealing with the World Bank—Shakertown, Inc., would have its financial problems solved and thus be able to achieve fully the objectives of the original EDA loan. Otherwise, "Shakertown would be struggling for years ahead to meet its obligations with marginal finances."

In response to his proposition, the EDA officials declared that the agency had no precedent for selling an asset at less than par value, nor did they have any precedent for settling a debt at less than par with a borrower in good standing (as Shakertown, Inc., was at the time). As part of his proposal, Wallace also asked that the EDA grant Shakertown a reasonable length of time to raise the money for the payment. His plan called for his old friends at the First National Bank of Louisville to purchase the note from the EDA and then, in turn, lend Shakertown, Inc., $750,000, on a one-year note, to buy it from the bank. He and the other trustees would then seek large contributions from tried-and-true donors and other friends of Pleasant Hill to free Shakertown from the debt.

Numerous meetings followed, one of them at Pleasant Hill in August 1978, when George Karras, the director of the EDA, inexplicably turned up to spend two days of what was supposed to be his vacation. In one of their talks, Wallace calmly told him that Shakertown "would most likely become a chronic defaulter." An old EDA hand who had followed the Shakertown loan from the beginning, Karras proved sympathetic to Wallace's aims. He and other officials had agreed that the project had accomplished more than they had hoped in improving the local economy, and they also conceded that if Shakertown had filed its application in 1962 instead of 1963, a good portion of the money would have come to it as an outright grant instead of as a loan (and thus would not have required repayment). The EDA officials also had no quarrel with Wallace's projections showing little improvement in the level of net income in the next years, and, he noted, "they see no sense in continually amending the contract with the prospect of the government's holding a note which might never be paid in full."

When Karras asked why Shakertown would try to raise $750,000 in a short time instead of putting on an annual fund drive to pay the interest on the note, Wallace gave him the facts of life on historic preservation, describing Shakertown as a "uniquely rural" institution with no public or civic constituency or support from the corporations and other enterprises that traditionally give to annual drives for the United Way, the Red Cross, hospitals, universities, and other institutions that chronically seek money. Besides, Wallace said, such a drive by Shakertown would signal distress at Pleasant Hill, and he had learned the general truth that large donors rarely wish to give money for expenses; that is, they much prefer building a building to helping pay the electric bill. Karras and his chief financial officer, Joe Hollister, another EDA veteran, also wondered why Wallace thought that

Shakertown might succeed in raising the $750,000. "I told them," Wallace
said, "I felt that our constituency and others might respond generously to a
'one-shot' effort to 'burn the mortgage.'"

After Hollister came to Louisville to meet with the bankers and Wallace
made further visits to Washington, the deal appeared to be working out.
For their part, the Shakertown trustees had voted Wallace the authority to
do whatever "in his sole judgment may be necessary or desirable" to achieve
the purpose. But then Hollister told Wallace that the EDA's general counsel was now holding the deal up, for two reasons. He believed that
Shakertown had valuable assets that could satisfy the EDA's claims, and
thus pay off the loan, if foreclosure should become necessary, and he had
reservations about the EDA's authority to sell the note at a discount when
Shakertown, Inc., was not actually in any financial difficulty, even though
it might have trouble in the future. A Michigan engineering firm appeared
at Pleasant Hill to survey the property in order to establish what it might
bring at a foreclosure auction.

Wallace and Bob Houlihan then went off to Washington for a conference with the general counsel. At this meeting Houlihan dashed any expectations the EDA lawyer might have entertained about the possibility of
seizing Shakertown's assets through a "deficiency judgment" following a
foreclosure by explaining the long, drawn-out legal problems such procedures faced in Kentucky. It also developed that an action to foreclose would
bring on a bureaucratic nightmare for the EDA in Washington, because a
National Historic Landmark could not be auctioned off without a series of
hearings and, besides, the announcement of such a sale would tend to de-
press the value of the property. "I reminded the EDA officials of this situation," Wallace said drily. Beyond that, if the government did take over the
property, it would have to operate it until the auction had taken place and
accounts were settled; that prospect pleased nobody. Thus Wallace held a
better hand than an observer might have thought.

The EDA general counsel's second point led to remarkable results. After explaining his doubts about the legality of "writing down" a loan asset
from $2,290,000 to $750,000—especially on an asset valued at far more
than the amount of the loan—the counsel responded to the very real pres-
sure to solve the problem with a statement of his own: the government

wanted to receive the whole amount of the loan plus the accrued simple interest, but it would be willing to wait for its money. Could Shakertown create a capital fund that would increase in value over time—it would have to equal $2,290,000 plus $83,012 a year for the interest—and thus settle the debt *eventually*. This suggestion amounted to a parallel route to the plan Wallace had proposed, since each called for the one-time raising of a fund that would, in effect and actually, eliminate the note from Shakertown's books.

Wallace saw the possibilities immediately and accepted the plan to set up such a fund, with the vitally important—the key—proviso that *at the same time the EDA would release the mortgage on the village*; the EDA officials agreed. This meant that the establishment of the capital fund would cancel all future payments on the loan; the EDA's money would come from this independent fund, not from Shakertown, Inc., and it would come all at once, decades in the future. For its part, the EDA thus chose to recover the entire principal and interest, even though it would not be forthcoming for many years, instead of now having to show on its books a loss of principal.

It was a paper victory for the EDA and a real-world triumph for Shakertown, and Wallace knew exactly how to achieve the goal. He and his financial assistant, Bill Walls, went to work to determine what size U.S. Treasury bond at what interest rate, compounded semiannually, would build up an amount sufficient to pay the interest and retire the loan in about twenty-five years. The bond would be put in a charitable trust to be administered by the First Kentucky Trust Company of Louisville.

It took numerous trips to Washington with spread sheets showing interest accumulations before the EDA would accept the proposal and the accompanying calculations as valid. As the lawyers drew up the various documents, Hollister asked where Shakertown would get the money for the original investment in the capital fund. No problem, Wallace replied in effect—they already had it, because they could borrow it from their endowment fund, which they could do legally as soon as the EDA released its mortgage on the village property. Of course, Wallace said, they would try to build up the endowment again. Who knew what adversities the future might hold?

There was one thing more: thanks to the wonders of compound interest, the amount required to produce the needed total, about $5 million, at $9^1/8$ percent was not $750,000 but only $420,000. For this sum, Shakertown, Inc., had now become free of a debt of more than $2 million. At one of the final meetings in Kentucky, one of the EDA representatives, watching Wallace's maneuvers, turned to Dr. Thomas Clark with a question: "How the hell did he do that?" Clark could only shrug. (It was certainly altogether fitting that in 1981, to celebrate the twentieth anniversary of Shakertown as a corporation, Wallace would play host to the ARA godfathers of the original loan that had made all the subsequent events possible—W. R. Abell, W. E. Davis, Charlie Dixon, and Jack Ingram.)

Wallace had "rifle vision," an associate said. "He would go straight to the completion of a project before you could talk to him about another project. When he would start a job, he never put it aside." Charlie Sturgill once observed that the "persistence and tenacity" Wallace always displayed in dealings on behalf of Shakertown were "beyond comprehension"; George Karras and Joe Hollister could certainly have given full testimony on that point. At the next meeting of the Shakertown board of trustees after the settlement of the loan issue, Thomas Spragens, the president of Centre College, expressed great admiration for Wallace's description of the transactions and dubbed him the "Pied Piper of Pleasant Hill." At the same meeting, Wallace announced that Shakertown, Inc., had just received a legacy of $200,000 from a supporter in Connecticut. Things were indeed looking up.

CHAPTER XI

"The Instruction of the Public"

❧

In 1965 Earl Wallace received an invitation to join some sixty other American leaders in politics, business, the professions, and the academic world at an American Assembly session titled "The Courts, the Public, and the Law Explosion." Established at Columbia University in 1950 by Dwight Eisenhower, then the university's president, the American Assembly was, and remains, a remarkable phenomenon, with its continuing nonpartisan conferences on public issues—usually two a year—at Arden House, the former family home of Averell Harriman on the edge of the Catskills fifty miles northwest of New York City.

Though deliberations at Arden House, with their carefully produced reports, have often influenced national thinking about policy, this well-intended 1965 session did little to dampen the spreading American enthusiasm for taking people to court. But that relative powerlessness was not apparent at the time, and in any case Wallace thoroughly enjoyed the meeting, taking part in discussions with the typical Arden House array of luminaries from various fields and coming away with "the feeling of having participated in something memorable and historic." In saying this, Wallace was expressing the reaction that most participants have to these meetings, which represent the truly top level of national-policy public discussion in the United States; once, a dazzled participant in another Arden House conference simply described himself as "floating." Wallace returned home with

the loftiest conceivable goal: he was determined to create a Kentucky version of Arden House at Pleasant Hill.

The idea of Pleasant Hill as the site of conferences and discussion of
course went back to the beginning days of the restoration, well before
Wallace's involvement with the project. When, guided by Raymond McLain,
the members of the Blue Grass Trust's Shakertown committee had concerned themselves with the question of the "proper usefulness" of a restored Pleasant Hill, they had concluded that only an important contribution
to society as a whole could justify the expenditure of time, effort, and money
the project would demand. The aim, McLain said, must be "to utilize the
property and facilities in such a manner as to improve the quality of contemporary life." The beauty of the setting, the founders believed, could
make perhaps its greatest contribution by enhancing the quality of thought
of those who came to study and deliberate.

McLain himself spoke of the "simplicity and discipline of the life lived
by the Shaker Community" as traits worthy of study and emulation, and,
indeed, it was on November 4, 1961—shortly after the creation of the
corporation and long before any material change at all had taken place at
Pleasant Hill—that Shakertown had made its first venture into the world
of conferences: "The Shaker Character: Does It Have Meaning for Today?"
The sponsors described the meeting, rather vaguely, as the first in a hoped-
for series of conferences on the history and culture of Shakertown as related to the growth of the United States.

With such activities in mind, however ill defined, the Shakertown trustees had made the decision to hire Ralph McCallister as the first executive
director, only to find that buildings had to come before programs and that
the miracle worker who could raise money, design the restoration, develop
and preside over conferences and educational activities, and keep the board
happy had not yet been born. Meeting in November 1963, the interim
education committee, chaired by Dorothy Clay of Bourbon County, one
of the hardest workers of all those involved with the project, decided that
"any definite recommendations for programs of education and recreation
would be premature at this point." Nevertheless, the group saw the "education project" as having at least three divisions: discussion by experts of
problems, issues, and trends of contemporary life; popular-level discus-

sions, on such topics as gardens, antiques, architecture, and art; and programs for professional groups for which Pleasant Hill would provide only the facilities. These points clearly reflected the distinction between making Pleasant Hill a vehicle for furthering the hopes and aims of the members themselves and using it simply as a hotel that would rent space to groups wanting to have meetings. With reference to the first two discussions, the committee noted that "a director familiar with this type of work should be employed" and added, mordantly, "This, in spite of our previous failure to select the right man."

In his speech at the opening of the restoration on May 31, 1964, McLain had made his almost mystical observations about how guests at the village would be able to see "life pared of its superficialities, yet see that it can remain beautiful because it is strong and neat and not gaudy." It was a few days afterward that Jim Cogar had told a questioner: "The whole idea is to make it a cultural and educational center." Waving his arm toward the rolling fields, Cogar said: "This could be a place where people come and settle in the peace and quiet of this area all sorts of problems. We hope to become international in scope."

While laboring over the application for the ARA loan, Earl Wallace had made sure to fold in his own version of the Pleasant Hill educational dream. For several years, since reading an article in the *Saturday Review* by the editor and writer Norman Cousins about the creation of the Aspen Institute for the Humanities in Colorado, Wallace had envisioned a similar center set in the Blue Grass. But he now saw one particular problem: Pleasant Hill held great promise, but would it really make sense to try to establish a conference center on a secondary highway in Mercer County, Kentucky, miles from any city? Would people be willing to come?

A chat with Cousins provided the answer Wallace hoped for. One reason for the popularity of Aspen and Columbia University's Arden House, Cousins pointed out, was precisely that these centers were not located in the middle of urban areas. Not tarrying, Wallace then added to his loan application a proposal for an "educational conference center"; having no specific plans to cite, he told the government that "the program contemplates a wide variety of panel discussions, conferences and seminars of subjects of an educational and cultural nature." Two years later, after attending the American Assembly, Wallace had seen for himself the advantages of bringing a group together in a rural setting, and for him creating a conference center had now become "an obsession."

But, aside from the question of what would actually take place in a conference center, a practical problem existed: Pleasant Hill had no suitable restored building to house such an activity. As far back as 1961, the Shakertown committee had envisioned the West Family group of buildings as the site of whatever educational activities might be developed; specifically, the two-story frame West Family Wash House would provide conference and assembly rooms. Until this restoration should take place, however, conferences would be limited in size and scope.

A meeting in October 1969 proved the point. Opening on Wednesday evening, October 22, a conference met for two days to discuss the future of the Ohio Valley; forty participants were on hand. The recently formed Ohio Valley Assembly—"a sort of regional chamber of commerce," said one reporter—served as the sponsor, with the Brookings Institution of Washington providing the intellectual leadership. Participants appeared to like Pleasant Hill, but Wallace noted the problems caused by "our present inadequate and inconveniently located facilities."

In 1972, the conference housing problem found its solution when Nettie Jones, who continued in the inner circle of Pleasant Hill's most devoted supporters, provided the funds to restore the West Family Wash House, a true eyesore. The most dilapidated building in the village, it had a large hole in the front wall through which farmers had brought tractors and other implements inside for repairs. The Wash House could now become a conference center, and the neighboring ten-room brick building, whose restoration Mrs. Jones also volunteered to fund, could offer lodging for overnight guests. As Wallace pointed out, Mrs. Jones had a special connection with the conference idea, since her late husband, a close friend of General Eisenhower, had played an influential part in establishing the American Assembly at Arden House.

The new center received its baptism from Thomas D. Clark, who from 1972 to 1974 conducted a series of colloquia on the U.S. Constitution and other subjects relating to public affairs. During this same time, Wallace was working with Philip Davidson, former dean of the graduate school at

Vanderbilt and former president of the University of Louisville, to develop
a possible approach to creating what Davidson, in June 1973, called "residential programs in continuing adult education of a liberal and humanistic
nature." Davidson did not stop with the humanities, however; he also suggested policy- and problem-oriented seminars, commenting that "it would
be easy to identify specific regional or state-wide problems that would be
worthwhile discussing." This seems to have been one of the first instances
of locally oriented, less-than-global thinking by anybody trying to design a
program of Pleasant Hill conferences.

Though most of the people involved believed that Pleasant Hill should
become a true educational conference center, what it should strive to accomplish in that role remained elusive. Yet, as Wallace reminded the trustees in October 1973, "Shakertown is incorporated as a nonprofit,
educational institution with purposes which qualify it for tax deduction of
gifts"; Davidson, he said, was continuing to consult on "ways we might
sponsor our own program and thus validate our original objective."
Davidson then produced two week-long versions of Aspen Institute seminars that brought the philosopher Mortimer Adler and the historian Jacques
Barzun to Pleasant Hill. No more erudite and stimulating discussion leaders could have been found in America, but this venture, for all its good
points, did not sharpen the focus for Pleasant Hill. What could take place
in the village that was not likely to happen anywhere else? What would be
special?

Constantly engaged in a search for persons of talent and achievement,
Wallace lived by the telephone. Characteristically, he responded to a magazine article or a radio or television discussion by calling the person whose
work he liked and arranging a lunch or a meeting at Pleasant Hill. Even
though Davidson's seminars did not lead to a continuing series of such
programs, the Barzun session indirectly brought about a new friendship for
Wallace that would have important consequences for Shakertown. After
watching *Comment on Kentucky,* a new Kentucky Educational Television
talk show on state politics presided over by Al Smith, then the publisher of
a weekly newspaper in Russellville, Kentucky, Wallace phoned Smith with
an invitation to attend the Barzun seminar, assuring him that it would cost
only $500. "My real feeling," Smith said years later, "was that I couldn't

afford five hundred dollars to spend a week at Pleasant Hill with Barzun— or maybe it was a couple of hundred dollars and it just seemed like five hundred." Smith contented himself, however, with telling Wallace that he couldn't take a week off from his various commitments.

Unperturbed at this turndown, Wallace telephoned Smith several months later with an invitation to a Kentucky Derby weekend at Pleasant Hill, with a box seat at the Derby included. The party proved to be a lavish affair, involving various notables and good talk before a blazing fire, and Wallace in future years delighted in pointing out that when the hospitality was free, Smith had eagerly accepted the invitation. "It was the first time I was ever at Shakertown," Smith said, "and it was one of the most unforgettable visits of my life. At the Derby, I couldn't believe I was having so much fun."

After that, Wallace invited Smith to Pleasant Hill numerous times, and the next year asked him to join the board of trustees. When Smith inquired about the length of the term of service, Wallace said, succinctly, "For life." This had in fact become the official policy of the corporation, adopted several years earlier when it became evident that, in cycling trustees off the board, Pleasant Hill was sacrificing much-needed dedication and knowledge. From that point on, Wallace and Smith developed a strong friendship, with Smith in regular attendance at Pleasant Hill events.

The first Shakertown Roundtable conference came in 1977. In August, starting the series off with a flourish, Wallace telephoned Averell Harriman, whose family had lived in Arden House and who thus uniquely symbolized the American Assembly. Wallace told the veteran statesman that Senator John Sherman Cooper and the Shakertown trustees had discussed creating a roundtable of Kentuckians "concerned about where this country is headed, politically, socially, and economically" and asked Harriman simply to speak to the first such meeting "on matters he thinks of great importance to us as a nation—in other words, to give us his perspective of our times."

This thoroughly global two-day visit earned wide newspaper and television coverage, and encouraged Wallace to invite James Reston, the renowned public-affairs columnist of the *New York Times,* to come to Pleasant

Hill for the 1978 Roundtable. In 1979, at the suggestion of Dillman A. Rash, a Shakertown trustee, Wallace brought in Herman Kahn, the pioneer futurist associated with the Hudson Institute in New York. During his two days at Pleasant Hill, Kahn dealt with world demographics of the twenty-first century and, justifying his futurist credentials, explained how the United States was changing from an industrial economy to an information society through dramatic advances in science and technology.

Each of these three conferences featured a star turn by a nationally eminent figure, and each was no doubt extremely interesting. But this did not prove to be the direction in which Pleasant Hill's future as a place of conferences would lie. The new outlook began taking shape one day in 1980, as Wallace, a constant and eclectic reader always hungry for facts, was looking over preliminary data from the new federal census. He became struck and then disturbed when he noted that the socioeconomic comparisons between Kentucky and Tennessee all seemed to go in Tennessee's favor.

It was one of Wallace's behavioral traits, particularly evident in his direction of the Roundtable, that it did not seem to occur to him that people would not do whatever he asked of them, and, in fact, rebellions had rarely arisen. He had built up a large and varied group of laborers in the Pleasant Hill vineyard who were always considered to be on call, and borrowing an old term, one of them, Tom Clark, referred to the members of the group as Wallace's "slave coffle," a coffle being a train of people, or animals, chained together by a master. After studying the census data, Wallace asked Philip Davidson, a key member of the coffle, to arrange a luncheon meeting in Nashville at which he could grill Vanderbilt economists and downtown bankers and businessmen on the reasons behind the differences between Kentucky and Tennessee. In essence, he wanted to know how Tennessee had been able to make so much more progress than Kentucky (in population growth, bank deposits, production of Ph.D.s) when its average per capita income was about the same as Kentucky's. The participants in this informal roundtable offered no explanation beyond saying that the existence of the Tennessee Valley Authority probably accounted for the difference. Wallace felt, however, that "the difference appeared to have involved something more fundamental than a few cents' cheaper electricity."

On returning home, Wallace telephoned Barry Bingham, certainly a willing worker if not an actually enchained member of the coffle, to set up a meeting for the two of them with Wilson Wyatt, former mayor of Louisville and lieutenant governor, to discuss a Shakertown Roundtable conference on a comparison of Kentucky and Tennessee. Here, at last, Pleasant Hill seemed to have found its role in the conference world: to focus not on the globe, not on the entire United States, but on Kentucky and the region. The meeting in Bingham's office, Wallace said, "gave birth to the present series of Roundtable conferences on subjects dealing with Kentucky's problems," and he accurately called it "a landmark meeting." The series continued unbroken for twenty-one years. The stationery of the organization long carried a statement of the Roundtable's role: "The instruction of the public on subjects useful to the individual and beneficial to the community." Few reading this simple definition were likely to realize that it came not from Wallace and his colleagues but directly from the chapter of the U.S. tax code setting out the requirements to be met by a tax-exempt educational corporation; it was, in surprisingly clear language, the bureaucratic equivalent of the Shakertown founders' term "proper usefulness."

The 1980 meeting established the format for Roundtable conferences; no longer solo performances by invited stars, they would now feature series of papers and analyses by students of the subject, with follow-up discussions. Inevitably, education took a prominent place on conference agendas, with the subject coming into sharp focus in the 1985 conference, "What Kentuckians Would Gain by Improving the State's Educational Standing." This topic emerged from a steering committee meeting in which the members agreed that a way must be found to convince the majority of Kentuckians that, as Wallace put it, "better schools would improve the chances of bringing in new plants and increasing the number of jobs. Otherwise, the majority of Kentuckian voters would continue their perception that improved education would not be worth the effort."

Speaking at this conference about the need to arouse public sentiment for improved schools, Barry Bingham gave the Roundtable its fundamental charge: "I think Kentucky desperately needs a 'gadfly' to keep persecuting Kentucky citizens on this subject. We just can't let them rest. We've got to do something on this, no matter if it takes one year, five years, ten years, for it to be effective. I see no other agency in the state of Kentucky that can do this except the Roundtable." The Binghams also did their part by providing consistent financial support.

To Bingham's charge, Michael Moloney, a state senator from Lexington, added: "I believe it is the goal of all of us who have discussed this so far to enable the Shakertown Roundtable to become the vehicle so needed in this state to provide some sense of direction for the future. The Roundtable bias must be a bias toward the improvement of the quality of life of Kentucky and of Kentuckians."

The very next year, the Roundtable took an intensely practical turn with a close examination of education in the Fifth Congressional District, in southeastern Kentucky. At the time this was the largest and most rural district east of the Mississippi, and, according to a story in *U.S. News and World Report*, it also had the lowest educational ranking of all 435 congressional districts. This stigma did not please the district's new congressman, Hal Rogers, nor did it sit well with Earl Wallace, who had been born and had received his early schooling in the district and who, as a firm and positive chairman, was ready to push discussion of the question. (As Davidson once commented, "Any time you've got Wallace, you've got a quorum of one. He knows how everything should be done.")

Following this conference, Wallace, passionately involved on behalf of his natal district, helped local leaders organize and obtain financial support for Forward in the Fifth, a nonpartisan school support group, headed by Joann and Ken James of London, that obtained funding to go into every county to improve school attendance, reduce dropouts, and reward teachers who are dedicated to the program. Results have been striking enough for Robert F. Sexton, director of the highly influential Prichard Committee for Academic Excellence, to call this probably the single most important result of the Shakertown Roundtable. "It got people together who could do something," he said, "and it inspired them. It had a very positive and very direct impact."

While the Roundtable did its part to stimulate statewide discussion of issues in education, great events were impending. In 1985, Bert Combs, on behalf of sixty-six relatively poor school districts, had filed a suit seeking to overturn the system of funding schools on the ground that the wide disparities between well-off districts and those that were property poor violated the state constitution. On May 31, 1988, before Wallace and his associates could adopt an agenda for the 1988 Roundtable conference, Judge Ray Corns of the Franklin Circuit Court handed down a decision destined for immediate fame: Combs, he said, had proved his case; the school system of the commonwealth was not "efficient," as the constitution requires. A comprehensive review of Corns's decision—wrapped into a package titled "The Tax Dollar in Kentucky: What Does It Buy?"—immediately became the agenda for the next Roundtable conference. Participants urged Governor Wallace Wilkinson and the legislature not to fight the decision but to implement it: as Earl Wallace sternly put it in a letter to the governor, "History will pronounce harsh judgment upon those of the present generation whose actions will continue to deprive Kentucky's school children of their educational birthright."

The result of all this was true history. The 1990 legislature adopted the now-famous Kentucky Education Reform Act, and national commentators immediately saw it as "the most sweeping educational package ever conceived by a state legislature." Albert Shanker, head of the New York Federation of Teachers, called the package "the most intelligent state reform program that has been adopted anywhere in the country." KERA, as the act and procedures under it became known, moved into domination of educational discussion in the state, a position it has held ever since, and, indeed, such discussion became far more common than ever before. At the 1985 Roundtable conference, Chester Finn of Vanderbilt, a former U.S. assistant secretary of education, had told participants that "successful educational reform must become an issue that ordinary people feel strongly about." That moment of feeling seemed finally to have come in Kentucky, as the result of many forces and currents, and a decade of discussion at Pleasant Hill—discussion that certainly fitted the founders' idea of proper usefulness—had played an important part. As Governor John Y. Brown had put it several years earlier, Shakertown was "a real thinking place."

Earl Wallace had such a strong identification with the Roundtable that persons who did not know the story tended to ascribe this side of Pleasant Hill entirely to his influence, not realizing all the soul-searching and defining of mission that had preoccupied the early committees; nor could such persons know that, in the eyes of the founders, the Roundtable, for all its success, would represent the fulfillment of only a small part of Pleasant Hill's social and intellectual mission.

The published report of the 1989 Roundtable conference, distributed in the spring of 1990, carried an announcement of the death of Earl Wallace, which occurred on April 3, 1990. He was ninety-one, and not long before, in conversation with friends about the need to tune up Kentucky's economy for the future, he had said, "What are we going to do about the twenty-first century?" His listeners had the feeling that he expected to be here to enjoy that century and to try to reform it. After Wallace's death, Al Smith urged the new Shakertown chairman, W. T. Young, to continue the Roundtable meetings, as did many other supporters, including Wilson Wyatt; Bob Doll, a Louisville attorney; and Tom Clark. Apart from their intrinsic merits, the public affairs activities at Pleasant Hill—especially the Shakertown Roundtable—had considerable publicity value, calling the village to the attention of persons who might otherwise give it little thought, as Young himself later noted with specific reference to the Roundtable. Similarly, Thomas commented that he saw "great value to the Shakertown Roundtable," which had "brought great renown to Shaker Village and has been good for Kentucky."

Smith and the other Roundtable advocates received a favorable hearing, and follow-up discussions led to the adoption of a leaner, stripped-down version of the meetings, lasting one day instead of two or more—a point that won the favor of both Young and Thomas; Smith, who had become the new Roundtable chairman, raised the money himself to pay for these conferences. Young liked the reformulated Roundtable, which Smith changed in more ways than simply its duration. He continued the practice of issuing thorough reports, but they now appeared as newsprint tabloids instead of Wallace's handsome, corporate-style publications. Kentucky Educational Television continued to support the programs, Smith noted, devoting an annual broadcast to them, and they continued to attract statewide coverage. But, said Smith, "noticeably diminished was participation by the Shakertown trustees, who seemed to follow the new leadership in focusing on the preservation mission and raising the money to pay for it."

On the other hand, Robert Sexton, who had become involved with the Roundtable in 1988 with his new organization the Kentucky Center for Public Issues, felt that, under Smith's direction, the Roundtable expanded its influence in the 1990s when the leadership began involving the press and inviting "more of a cross-section of Kentucky, people who could use the information and take it some place." Sexton also praised Smith's innovation of commissioning articles and distributing them to newspapers across the state. The Roundtable in the 1990s, Sexton thought, was more directly practical than previously because it was planned to be practical.

At its best, the Roundtable served as the gadfly Barry Bingham had sought for confronting issues important to Kentucky. Sessions in the 1990s dealt with such topics as tax questions, the condition of local government, the accountability of public schools, and the future of private higher education in the commonwealth. At the end of the decade, Al Smith announced his retirement as chairman of the Roundtable. "I think Bill Young sincerely appreciated Al's swan song, which was a remarkable ending to his chairmanship," Thomas said. "I thought we were going to have a meeting like the other meetings, and then Al said, 'No, I need a budget of $30,000,' and it [Smith's last roundtable] ended up at more than $70,000—all of which he raised. To his credit, it came off beautifully."

What Thomas was describing here was a colossal multistage event developed in great detail by Smith over a number of months in 1999, with the theme: "Kentucky Leaders for the New Century." Early in the year, Smith, in collaboration with Pam Luecke, then the editor of the *Lexington Herald-Leader,* and two dozen other editors across the state, had launched a search for persons under the age of forty with high potential to be leaders of the commonwealth in the twenty-first century. From 338 nominees, the selection panel chose forty-four to take part in preliminary sessions at state parks, at the Roundtable meeting at Pleasant Hill in November, and in discussions during the ensuing year. The Roundtable agenda, as one might expect, focused on what looked to be the most pressing challenges that would face the state in the coming years, with emphases on education, environmental, and growth issues.

Smith conceived of the program as a way to develop more grassroots efforts aimed at solving problems and also to create an intellectual climate encouraging to new ideas, but, though this 1999 new leaders' Roundtable won wide attention across the Commonwealth, the Shakertown administration did not accept a series of recommendations Smith submitted for continuing the Roundtable after his retirement. In fact, in 2000, for the first time in more than twenty years, no Roundtable conference was held at Pleasant Hill. With Wallace gone and Smith now out of the picture, such activities had lost their founder and their strongest advocate. The future of public affairs discussion at Pleasant Hill did not look promising. A look behind the scenes will clarify the picture.

CHAPTER XII

The Restoration Restored

❧

Despite his advanced age, Earl Wallace had continued his uninterrupted close supervision of the Pleasant Hill operation until the weekend he died. Just a few days earlier—proving that he did not always insist on adding property to the Shakertown holdings—he had closed his last deal, which involved the sale of 1,431 acres of farmland (given in the 1970s by Pansy Poe) and added $1 million to the village endowment, doubling it. Without Wallace, said Wilson Wyatt, "Shakertown wouldn't exist." "He was Shakertown," added Philip Davidson. "Everybody understood that."

But, in fact, everybody did not understand it. The dissenters even included Shakertown's president since 1975, Jim Thomas, who might well have agreed with the view that Wallace was Shakertown in earlier years but felt that during the latter 1980s the chairman had devoted excessive attention—and money—to the development of the Shakertown Roundtable, at the expense of day-to-day maintenance of the village and of needed updating of the infrastructure. Thomas even cited a somewhat less-than-glowing 1989 restaurant review in the *Lexington Herald-Leader*.

Wallace was not "embarrassed" by problems with the physical plant and hence was disinclined to remedy them, according to Thomas; hence roofs, mechanical systems, and ventilating and other equipment of all kinds had deteriorated badly and even become obsolete in the 1980s. Made an ardent preservationist by his experience first in Louisville and then through

the years of close association with Jim Cogar at Pleasant Hill, Thomas concluded that Wallace had simply lost interest in the Shaker Village as an
outdoor museum. "He disdained the use of the word 'museum,'" Thomas
recalled, "and prohibited the staff from using the word."

In moving the emphasis at the village to conferences, specifically the
Roundtable, Thomas said, Wallace brushed aside the preservation and education advocates on the staff and grew testy with their pleas for support. He
eliminated the funds for staffing the library, for acquiring primary and
secondary source materials, and for periodicals, Thomas remembered.
This unhappy time found Thomas and Ed Nickels, then the director of
collections, using their own money to buy needed materials and mem-
berships in professional organizations so that the library would receive
their publications. Staff travel was eliminated from the budget, as the
increasingly autocratic chairman ruled that staff members who attended
professional meetings during the week, at their own expense, would lose
vacation time.

The last annual report on the village itself, Thomas noted, was written
by Wallace in 1979. During the 1980s, the chairman focused on producing glossy reports about the Roundtable, a practice that was discontinued
after Wallace's death when Thomas reactivated the annual reports to include preservation and educational programs and progress in village activities.

Although Wallace would not spend money on such items as Shaker
furniture, Thomas finessed that obstacle in 1984 by winning a $250,000
grant from the James Graham Brown Foundation for furniture purposes.
Also in the 1980s, despite Wallace's cooling interest in scholarly conferences on preservation, Thomas convened and chaired meetings that
brought to Pleasant Hill representatives from Old Sturbridge, Deerfield,
and similar historic villages. Thomas left no doubt that in the conflict
between those primarily interested in the historic legacy of the village
itself and those who saw it just as much as a setting for a variety of educational and cultural activities, he gave preservation an emphatic Number
One priority.

Outside the Pleasant Hill circle during the 1980s, preservationists had
taken a highly favorable view of Wallace's performance. In 1985, at the age

of eighty-six, the chairman saw his efforts in behalf of Shakertown win recognition across the country as well as at home, as he received the medal for historic preservation from the Garden Clubs of America and the John Wesley Hunt award from the Blue Grass Trust. But behind the scenes at Pleasant Hill, the board of trustees had long harbored an anti-Wallace faction, or, at least, a group that only reluctantly acquiesced in the chairman's direction of village affairs. Wallace had plenty of supporters, however, and his prestige remained enormous among people who could look back two decades and more to days when the fledgling Pleasant Hill project had been widely derided as "Wallace's Folly." Such factors, together with the chairman's well-known dominating personality and assertive management style, meant that he continued, unchallenged, in charge of affairs, even into his nineties.

Regardless of the tensions and dislikes that had existed at the top, Wallace's death confronted Shakertown's trustees with a problem they had not faced since 1961, when Wallace had become temporary chairman of the incorporators of Shakertown at Pleasant Hill; his supposedly short-time tenure had lasted from those shaky, penniless days, when many had considered the restoration little more than an impossible dream, through twenty-nine years that had seen Shakertown achieve national recognition as a historic village. The choice of Wallace's successor, however, came as no surprise to anybody. William T. Young of Lexington had joined the Shakertown board in 1985 ("as you get older you become available to work on some of these things") and had later been persuaded by Wallace to serve as vice chairman, which, Young said, "was the same as putting the finger on me when he died." Thus Wallace had regarded Young as his heir presumptive, and at the June board meeting the trustees confirmed the selection.

The new chairman, who was seventy-two, expressed some initial surprise at this turn of events. "I never really anticipated being chairman," he said. "I really thought Earl Wallace would live forever"—a view, one feels, that to some extent was shared by Wallace himself. Like his predecessor, Young had no particular devotion to the Shakers but admired Pleasant Hill and the achievement of those who had preserved it, and he fully believed in its importance for the Blue Grass area and the entire state of Kentucky. If the Shakertown trustees wanted an astute businessman in the chairman's seat, they could hardly have made a better choice. As many observers commented, Young, a trim gentleman with a dash of elegance, seemed to have a golden touch in every sphere of activity, from peanut butter to storage and hauling to soft drinks to thoroughbreds; for some time he held the largest single block of stock in the Humana corporation. No special touch at all, Young once declared: "You can take any business, and if you just do a little better job, you'll succeed." That approach produced remarkable results in the racing world, in which Young, who entered it at sixty, saw to it that he had the best people working for him and went on to breed thoroughbreds that won the Breeders' Cup and all three legs of the Triple Crown.

Involved as he was in a variety of businesses and philanthropies, Young made it plain that he would not seek to duplicate Wallace's absorption in the minutiae of Pleasant Hill. "Mr. Wallace devoted 100 percent of his time to it," he said. "That would be hard for me to do." Instead, after meetings involving the board and staff, the board approved Young's plan to divide Wallace's position in two, with Jim Thomas retaining his title as president and now, as chief executive officer, acquiring the operational responsibilities that normally go with the title. This arrangement pleased both men. Aside from the limits on his own time, Young preferred an administrative structure in which the board, while having its own responsibilities, was separate from the chief executive. The new CEO, who had essentially functioned as museum curator under Wallace's chairmanship, now had the opportunity he had long desired to spread his administrative wings. "Mr. Wallace was a very hands-on person, very involved in Shakertown in every way. Mr. Young is more of a traditional chairman," Thomas told a reporter. "I'm a good chairman," Young summed up years later. "I don't interfere with anybody."

Now that he had a new chairman to work with, Thomas made the most of the opportunity to explain his views and concerns, and Young proved to be a receptive listener. "After a lot of conversation and due study of the operation," as Thomas summed it up, "Bill Young decided that we needed to reaffirm the mission of the corporation. This mission is basically the preservation and interpretation of this remarkable national landmark site." Young soon moved to appoint "an ad hoc committee to assess long-term facility needs at the village," chaired by Edie Bingham and Sally Brown, which produced a comprehensive list of overall priorities for the village. Underlying the list was its call for a new mission statement and long-range plan "designed to place the highest institutional priority on education and interpretation." Recommendations included strengthening the core interpretation programs and developing an interpretive plan, "articulating the primary themes and messages Shakertown wants to convey"; the village also needed to improve orientation for visitors. On the physical side, the buildings should be evaluated and documented, and, in fact, archaeologists should conduct a survey of the entire village site, thus making more knowledge available for practical use—with visitors always in mind. Reflecting Thomas's worry about the Shakertown collections, the committee called for fresh emphasis on proper storage and documentation.

Young then chose Edie Bingham to lead a long-range planning committee that would, in effect, assign priorities to the priorities and show how they could be turned into realities. One means of accomplishing that goal, of course, would be money. Young adopted a policy of reinvesting all the income from Shakertown's $2 million endowment, using none of it for current operations. The chairman also pushed the endowment committee to invest in stocks, and indeed he had the times with him: during the 1990s the endowment would grow to more than $10 million.

In 1991, conveniently marking the thirtieth anniversary of the incorporation of Shakertown at Pleasant Hill, the Young administration launched a capital campaign, the first such effort since Wallace's differently focused drive in the 1970s to raise money to cover the interest on the government loan. Now the drive came in response to the problems with the village infrastructure that for several years had perturbed Thomas. Whatever the differences in outlook at Pleasant Hill had been, the restoration was now a generation old and clearly needed renewing.

"We found Shakertown almost in crisis," said Bob Warren, vice president of Bill Young's company (when you acquired Young's services in an endeavor of any kind, you also acquired "Young, Inc."). Warren, a former Kentucky state finance director, continued, "There were two urgent needs—renovation and capital—and this was in the face of declining tourism." Beyond taking basic steps in these areas, since "visitation was going down and we had to do something," the administration undertook a thorough study of the dining operations, with the result that ways were found to save some $200,000 a year. For one thing, the long-established no-tipping policy was abolished, which meant that patrons would in effect pay an increased share of staff wages—an important consideration, since the figures showed that labor costs amounted to two-thirds of revenue. In another change of policy, the village began accepting credit cards, a move Wallace had been reluctant to make, chiefly because he objected to paying the required fees to the issuers of the cards. Though his attitude seemed anachronistic in 1990, he had not been wholly idiosyncratic in holding it; Colonial Williamsburg, the national paradigm of historic restoration, had resisted the cards just as long and had made the switch at just about the same time as Shakertown. The village also adopted a long-deferred handicapped-accessibility project, a development Wallace had opposed—on puristic grounds, some friends believed, though Thomas said that Wallace simply "didn't want to spend the money"; here the tide of history clearly and irresistibly ran in the other direction. And in the new restoration careful planning cleverly concealed the lifts for handicap access, as was the case with the other modern features. Bob Warren went on to develop "a deep understanding of the fiscal aspect of the Shaker Village," Thomas said, and as liaison with Young he proved to be "a superb colleague, helpful in every area."

By 1993, Young had proved himself to be a formidable fund-raiser on behalf of Shakertown—the capital campaign ended with a total of $5,528,818, exceeding the $5 million goal. The chairman proved particularly persuasive in dealing with wealthy members of the board, several of whom made contributions in the $250,000 range. Beyond paying for the needed physical changes, some of the money would go to the development of new interpretive programs; following the recommendations of a committee on interpretive work, the Shakertown board created two new positions, education specialist and historic farm specialist. The holders of these posts developed the Shaker Life exhibit, showing the role of the Believers' religious convictions and the functioning of their families, and the historic farm program, which explored and presented the Shakers' remarkable agricultural expertise, featuring live animals with, as one observer said, "sights, sounds, and smells."

The realm of interpretation made a major advance through the work of Kim McBride of the University of Kentucky, whose archaeological survey, begun in the summer of 1990, located the foundations of many original buildings, of which thirty-four survive. The dramatic find here came in 1997, when McBride and her colleague, Philippe Chavance, a French architect, found the long-sought Shaker outdoor secret worship center called Holy Sinai's Plain, a half-acre site about half a mile from the center of the village, which had proved elusive because the Shakers, after the 1840s, had disguised it as ordinary farmland. "The location of this holy field," declared the elated McBride, "is something that has eluded researchers for more than thirty years."

McBride's dig did not represent the first archaeological efforts at Pleasant Hill. During the 1970s, some fifteen years earlier, a grant from the Lilly Endowment had funded a search, carried out over three summers, by a Centre College professor, Don Janzen, with the help of students, for the sites of the grist and other mills a mile down the hill from the village on the creek called Shawnee Run. Janzen, an enthusiastic practitioner of his professional discipline who continued to lead occasional archaeological tours of the village through the 1990s, had his own lively specialist views on historic preservation. He saw the restored beautiful and serene Pleasant Hill of the 1840s as entirely too much of a pristine package; for him, crumbled walls and fragments of pillars and posts in the village ought to have been left in their just-excavated state to serve as archaeological testaments to the passage of time. This view seems kin to that of a current writer on restoration, Howard Mansfield, for whom "good restoration should contain its opposite: going away, softening, decay." (The curators at Colonial Williamsburg apparently had similar feelings when they decided to restore horse manure to the village streets.)

The drive for land and buildings had continued during the later years of Earl Wallace's chairmanship, with the 1986 purchase of a neighboring 480-acre farm having brought back into the fold the last remaining group of original buildings, about a mile from the center of the village, known as the West Lot. Restored and opened for use in 1988, the West Lot dwelling became the new center for large conferences such as Roundtable meetings, and in 1990 a grant from the James Graham Brown Foundation, Kentucky's largest foundation, provided $500,000 to finish the restoration of that particular building complex, including the West Lot Wash House, which was completed in 1992. (This very generous foundation took its name from a colorful Louisville multimillionaire who lived in a simple suite in his own hotel, suitably named the Brown, and was known as the richest man in Kentucky at the time of his death in 1969.)

Young was convinced by Thomas that they should continue the land drive, beginning in 1991 with the purchase of a two-acre tract, with two side-by-side houses fronting on Highway 33, half a mile from the village. Like various earlier acquisitions, this represented a defensive move against the possibility of those houses turning into dreaded gas stations, the fear that had haunted the founders in the 1960s. In 1997, the administration purchased a 101-acre tract colorfully known as the back Teater farm (to distinguish it from its neighbor, the front Teater farm), bordering the northwest corner of the West Lot and providing access to the Chinn-Poe Nature Preserve, located on the mouth of Shawnee Run at its junction with the Kentucky River. The chief virtue of this acquisition lay in the opportunity it gave Shakertown to increase the diversions it could offer visitors by developing hiking and horseback-riding trails; two years later twelve miles of trails were opened to the public, and eventually the total rose to forty.

From a preservationist point of view, two building projects earned much comment, in good part because of their deceptive nature. The new administration building, opened in 1994, stands next to the Trustees' House parking lot and thus just on the edge of the restored area; the illusion comes from the fact that the building looks exactly like a black tobacco barn and, as such, attracts so little attention that it almost seems not to be there. During the next year came the "Building within a Building," the new concrete-block research library and collections repository built inside an actual tobacco barn, also painted black. "The barn has been part of the village landscape for fifty or sixty years," Thomas said at the time, "and we wanted to keep it that way." The idea for the latter project, Thomas said, came from Young himself.

In 1999, the Shakertown administration honored the memory of Dot Clay, who had died during the year, by establishing the Dorothy Norton

Clay Furniture Collection. In one move, Thomas was able to make up the earlier arrears in the assembling of original Shaker furniture and accessories from Pleasant Hill by the acquisition of an outstanding collection, numbering sixty-three pieces, from Mrs. Hazel Hamilton of nearby Buena Vista, in Garrard County, Kentucky; $149,000 toward the purchase came from board members and family and friends of Mrs. Clay, who had not only worked hard for Shakertown for many years but, as Earl Wallace once noted, had been the largest Kentucky contributor to the project. The Brown Foundation, which had become a good friend indeed of Pleasant Hill, granted an additional $50,000 for the cause.

Dominant among the concerns of the administration and the board at the beginning of the third millennium was the future of Pleasant Hill itself, caught up in what Thomas called "the struggle preservationists face to keep up public interest, awareness, and support at a time when historic sites are experiencing attendance declines. There is a problem, and the efforts of staff and trustees to cope with it are ongoing."

In May 2000, saying that he wanted to unclutter his life, William T. Young announced his resignation as chairman of Shakertown at Pleasant Hill, Inc., and retired, leaving the village "physically and financially in pristine condition"; after a life marked by extraordinary success in many fields of activity, Young would die four years later at the age of eighty-four. Alex Campbell, a Lexington businessman and close friend whom Young had picked as vice chairman of the Shakertown trustees and thus as his heir presumptive, took over as chairman. In his youth Campbell had been close to Earl Wallace, who, Young said, "was almost like a daddy to him," giving the succession almost a dynastic quality. With reference to Campbell's new responsibilities at Pleasant Hill, "I just told Alex not to let it deteriorate," Young said. "It's a Kentucky gem, and it should be preserved forever."

CHAPTER XIII

Pleasant Hill Frescoes

❧

W e want you to take in everything," says the interpreter in the full-skirted costume, urging us to attend the session of Shaker song and then the discussion of theology before returning to the Centre Family House for the tour. "The architecture and the furnishings are interesting, and the way they lived is interesting, too."

Although we appreciate her friendly suggestions, we decide to poke in elsewhere and see what goes on in the various demonstration areas before coming back in an hour. . . .

We walk over to the East Family Wash House, where we see the original "arches"—the cauldrons in which the Shaker women (yes, the women did the laundry) boiled the water they used—and the clever devices that protected the women from burns. "Each family dwelling had its own wash house," the demonstrator explains. "The sisters here would be washing for about seventy or eighty people. You always got your own clothes back from the laundry; you had your initials on everything." Pointing to the tubs, she says that "they washed in one and rinsed in the other. They changed jobs the first Saturday of every month, so they didn't always do the laundry." Thus a woman might spin or weave one month and do laundry duty the next. . . .

In a neighboring shop we meet the "silk ladies," who tell us about caterpillars and silkworms, and buttress their discussion by displaying tiny eggs for the incubation of these valuable worms. "You can put lots and lots of them in a small mason jar," says one of the silk ladies; she's right—there are hundreds of them inside. The end result of this animal farming will be beautiful, soft-hued yarn. . . .

We chat with another craftsman, the village cooper, who is finishing up a noggin as we come in and tells us all about noggins, piggins, and firkins—all the buckets of different sizes the Shakers made and used. As he taps away with his hammer while talking about the practical habits of the Shakers, he comments that "there are things you just can't get out of a book." In Shaker days, he says, the shop turned out a couple of thousand pieces a year—a good record. "Just sitting down and making something like a spoon out of a good piece of wood," he says, "gives me a satisfying feeling.". . .

We move along to the East Family Brethren's Shop, and right away we are watching and listening carefully as a craftsman makes a delicate oval box, explaining each step as he proceeds. "What I'm doing," he tells his audience, "is trying to copy what the Shakers were doing. By the 1840s and '50s they had monopolized the market, and all those little boxes they made became known as the Shaker box. By the end of the Civil War they had been replaced by tin cans, and the boxes were relegated to the gift shop." This craftsman bases himself in the 1840s, and we learn, for example, that though sandpaper was known at the time, it was little used; the Shakers did the job with scrapers. . . .

Then, across the hall, we watch an elderly and very enthusiastic craftsman show his audience how the Shakers made brooms. "What they didn't sell around here," he says, "they put on a boat and sent down the river, all the way to New Orleans." These brooms were, of course, among the most famous and popular of all the Shaker products. Using machines that look like nothing you ever saw, the broommaker displays impressive deftness, and something about the smell of the broom grass gives the experience a special touch of authenticity. . . .

In the East Family Sisters' Shop we hear discussion of the finer points of spinning and weaving. . . . We walk along to the Farm Deacon's Shop to look at the display of Shaker herbs and hear how the Believers used them and packaged and sold them. . . . We go into the Water House, remembering how it was restored on the impetus of Pansy Poe and again, as everywhere in the village, admiring the ingenuity set free by the Shaker view of the world. . . .

Returning to the Centre Family House, we make up part of a group that receives a thorough tour from bottom to top, seeing in particular how the Shakers used space to fill a large building with light and air.

Later, by the craft store, a tiny detail reminds us how everything in the Shaker world had its place in an established order—the wrought-iron gate handles opposite the latch spiral inward gracefully. This is beauty, but it is practical beauty, in the Shaker tradition: a latch like this will not catch on your clothes as you pass. Here, we see, not only in the forms of the buildings, the furniture, and the tools, but in everything the design has a purpose. Witness the gentle curves of the twin staircases in the Trustees' House that spiral upward—while the absence of supporting columns maximizes space on the ground level.

Had we planned it, we could take a one-hour river cruise on Pleasant Hill's sternwheeler *Dixie Belle,* observing the flora and fauna of the river's towering palisades, and we recall having heard that at a dinner honoring Earl Wallace many years earlier, Jim Thomas presented the chairman with a cap signaling his position as a Kentucky River commodore. Even without that nautical diversion, however, all those accomplished and articulate craftspersons have given us quite a full afternoon.

We notice how often we hear people speaking of Pleasant Hill use the word "serenity." Some of this feeling surely comes from the classical sense of order and proportion—balance, clarity, restraint, unity, and reason—the Shakers brought to their work of building. As we look up and down the village street, open spaces and solid buildings create a slow, rhythmic pattern, first with the neat line of alternating architecture and green space along the path itself, which is then echoed by the buildings set back from the road. The materials themselves, along with the buildings etched against the sky, appear solid and linear. Especially striking is the sharp, horizontal pattern of dark against light created by the sun on clapboards, with each board underscored by its own black shadow.

Perhaps all this order, and its accompanying serenity, account for one of the most remarkable aspects of life at Pleasant Hill. Despite all the comments everyone makes about Shakers' peculiar views on domestic life, Pleasant Hill seems to have been an extraordinarily healthful place to live. I learn from a book by Jim Thomas and his brother Sam, *The Simple Spirit,* that in the 1840s, according to the calculation of Micajah Burnett, the Believers at Pleasant Hill had an average life expectancy of seventy-one— before the discovery not only of antibiotics but even of microbes; from the *World Almanac* I then learn that the United States as a whole would not reach this figure for another 125 years.

Perhaps a visiting reporter understood something about this. "For the Shakers, the dual entrances and stairways that separated the sexes create a symmetry and order that is supremely soothing," wrote Allen Breed of the Associated Press. "You fall asleep to the lowing of milk cows and awake to the cooing of mourning doves."

Perhaps, then, that Greyhound bus driver back in 1957 had a sound point about the separation of the sexes. Or perhaps the simple beauty of Pleasant Hill was its own reward.

A Note on Jim Thomas's Service

Al Smith

❧

Soon after Earl Wallace's death in 1990, his successor as chairman of the Shakertown board, W. T. Young, told friends that he liked Jim Thomas's ideas about what needed to be done next. Young also said he trusted Thomas's administrative skills, which he thought had been underutilized by Wallace. Then, leaving the hands-on management of Shakertown to Thomas, as chief executive officer, Bill Young enlisted additional trustees to back a new endowment campaign that brought in more than $5.5 million.

Just as Wallace had attracted generous financial gifts from prominent women, Bill Young, who also had the social graces, began to call on the ladies who could write checks and to solicit advice from women such as Edie Bingham of the Louisville media family, who became Shakertown's first female vice chairman.

Another "first" for women occurred with Jim Thomas's recommendation of Madge Adams as his successor when he announced in the spring of 2004 that he would retire the following year. Young's successor as chairman, Alex Campbell, endorsed and the trustees duly elected Thomas's choice of Adams, the comptroller and vice president, to be the new president and CEO.

Bill Young died in 2004, leaving Campbell, Thomas, Adams, and the trustees to face an unresolved serious problem—the challenge of a decline in visits to Shakertown and other historic sites across the country. Places like Colonial Williamsburg, George Washington's Mount Vernon, Andrew Jackson's Hermitage, and a Massachusetts Shaker site, Hancock Village, experienced steep drops in attendance, and so did Shakertown. Lower attendance resulted in lower revenues. As trustees reluctantly tapped the $9 million endowment fund to cover shortfalls, Campbell launched a Save Shakertown Forever Fund, persuading seven trustees to follow his lead with $250,000 gifts each. He then set about expanding the endowment, which is the ultimate safety net for any institution.

As Chairmen Young and Campbell tilted the mission back to preservation, it slights none of the other active trustees to note that they and Thomas received extra encouragement from one particular trustee, Ralph Anderson, the CEO of the Belcan Engineering Group in Cincinnati. Anderson had taken a special interest in Shakertown when he was developing a large farming operation in his native Mercer County. Reflecting his confidence in Thomas, in particular, Anderson's financial gifts to Shakertown included a new information technology system and the acquisition of nearly one hundred acres of adjoining property that included the site of the famous Kissing Bridge.

While Thomas prepared to step aside for Madge Adams, he could review with much pride the award-winning accomplishments of his tenure: the addition of forty miles of hiking, riding, and carriage trails, the construction of administrative and archival buildings, the installation of facilities to accommodate the disabled, other positive changes in the physical plant and the thirty-five historic buildings, plus a year-round calendar of recreational and cultural attractions for visitors.

Although Earl Wallace had a policy of paying county taxes as a gesture of goodwill and support to Mercer County, Thomas negotiated a reversal of this with the county under the reasonable point that Shakertown is a not-for-profit educational institution. In a time that demanded change, this move saved Shakertown hundreds of thousands of dollars.

It takes nothing from the achievements of the formidable Earl Wallace, who was my dear friend and mentor, to conclude that with the unstinting support of Wallace's successors, Young and Campbell, and their trustees, Jim Thomas had actually restored the restoration of Shakertown, and expanded it. He had also survived his frustrations with the aging Wallace of the 1980s to the point that when Thomas's retirement was announced, he had replaced Wallace as Kentucky's most respected executive in the field of historic preservation.

Journalist Al Smith, a trustee of Shakertown since 1976, was chairman of the Shakertown Roundtable, 1990–2000.

Sources and Background

❧

The essential sources for establishing the timing and sequence of events were contemporaneous documents—the minutes of the Blue Grass Trust for Historic Preservation and of its Shakertown Committee, the minutes of the Board of Trustees of Shakertown at Pleasant Hill, Inc., and the minutes of the Executive Committee of the Board of Trustees. These, together with reports, memoranda, letters, budgets, and other such documents of the time, provided the thread of the narrative. This material came from the Department of Special Collections of the University of Kentucky Libraries, from several large boxes stored at Shakertown, and from the files of the late Robert F. Houlihan, attorney for the Shakertown board. Also important were narratives written by Earl Wallace: "Shakertown at Pleasant Hill," "The Shakertown Roundtable," and an untitled typescript of accounts of events during the restoration of the Shaker Village.

As quotations throughout the book show, much important information, with many insights and details, came from interviews and more informal conversations with persons who had various kinds of involvement with the Shaker Village and its restoration. The list includes Hilary J. Boone Jr., Jimmie Campbell, the late Thomas D. Clark, Richard DeCamp, Joseph C. Graves Jr., Carolyn Hammer, Susan Jackson Keig, the late Clay Lancaster, Vivian Landrum, Bettye Lee Mastin, Dixie Moore, Betty W. Morris, the late Louie B. Nunn, Evalina Settles, Robert F. Sexton, Al Smith, the late Betty Tenney, James C. Thomas, Bob Warren, the late William T. Young, and one person who wishes to remain anonymous. Also valuable were two video productions, Kentucky Educational Television's tribute to Earl Wallace in the *Distinguished Kentuckian* series and Shakertown's own *Shaker Images* production, "James Lowry Cogar: A Living Tribute," and an audiotape from Shakertown files of an interview with Cogar.

Fortunately, the restoration of the Shaker Village received extensive continuing coverage in area newspapers. I drew on the *Courier-Journal*, the *Harrodsburg Herald*, and the *Lexington Herald* (later the *Lexington Herald-Leader*) for a number of descriptive details that would have been long lost without their careful attention.

With reference to the Shaker background as given in chapter 2 and chapter 3: Some of this information came from research material prepared at Shakertown early in the restoration project. In addition, of the many books that have been written about the Shakers, I found the following especially useful: *Maps of the Shaker West: A Journey of Discovery,* by Martha Boice, Dale Covington, and Richard Spence (Dayton, Ohio: Knot Garden Press, 1997); *Pleasant Hill and Its Shakers,* by Thomas D. Clark and F. Gerald Ham (Pleasant Hill, Ky.: Shakertown Press, 1968); *Noble But Plain,* by Jerry V. Grant (Old Chatham, N.Y.: Shaker Museum and Library, 1994); *Old Shakertown and the Shakers,* by Daniel Mac-Hir Hutton (Harrodsburg, Ky.: Harrodsburg Herald Press, 1936); *A Walking Tour of Shakertown,* by Bettye Lee Mastin, with illustrations by Patricia S. DeCamp (Lexington, Ky.: Richard S. DeCamp, 1969); *The Shakers and the World's People,* by Flo Morse (Hanover, N.H.: University Press of New England, 1987 [reissue of 1980 Dodd, Mead, and Company edition]); *The Story of the Shakers,* by Flo Morse (Woodstock, Vt.: The Countryman Press, 1986); *The Kentucky Shakers,* by Julia Neal (Lexington: University Press of Kentucky, 1977); *The Simple Spirit,* compiled by Samuel W. Thomas and James C. Thomas (Pleasant Hill, Ky.: Pleasant Hill Press, 1973); *Education and Recreation of the Shakers,* by Sister Miriam Wall (East Canterbury, N.H.: Canterbury Shakers, n.d.). *The Shakers and the World's People,* from which I drew several comments, is a particularly valuable anthology of material about the Shakers and was well described by one reviewer as "an indispensable storehouse." I also received useful material from my friend Theodore Levitt, editor emeritus of the *Harvard Business Review.* In addition to the books mentioned here, those interested in further reading might also wish to take a look at *The Shaker Experience in America,* by Stephen J. Stein (New Haven, Conn.: Yale University Press, 1992).

For the discussion of the evolution of historic preservation in the United States and differing points of view concerning it, I drew—aside from conversations with James Thomas, Betty Morris, and others—on a number of books, including *Antebellum Houses of the Bluegrass,* by Clay Lancaster (Lexington: University of Kentucky Press, 1961); *Changing Places,* by Richard Moe and Carter Wilkie (New York: Henry Holt and Company, 1997); *Keeping Time,* by William J. Murtagh (New York: John Wiley and Sons, 1997); *1929: America before the Crash,* by Warren Sloat (New York: Macmillan, 1979); and *Presenting the Past,* an anthology edited by Susan Porter Benson, Stephen Brier, and Roy Rosenzweig (Philadelphia: Temple University Press, 1986). Also, an interested reader might enjoy Cabell Phillips's portrait of Colonial Williamsburg, "The Town That Stopped the Clock," in *American Heritage* (February 1960). Other useful material included an unpublished paper, "The Blue Grass Trust for Historic Preservation Backgrounder," by Greg Rinhart (provided by the Blue Grass Trust).

Earl Wallace's personal narratives had special value in providing sidelights on his complex financial dealings on behalf of Shakertown, as described in chapters 8 and 10. Those wishing to look further into the workings of the bond market might consult a most interesting book, *The Life and Times of Dillon Read,* by Robert Sobel (New York: Truman Talley Books/ Dutton, 1991).

For making books, clippings, and other materials available to me, I am grateful to Joseph C. Graves Jr.; Donna Moore, of Kentucky Educational Television; the late Betty Tenney, daughter of Earl Wallace; and Marnie Gregory Walters, then director of the Blue Grass Trust for Historic Preservation. I also owe a considerable debt to staff members of the Special Collections and Digital Programs of the University of Kentucky Libraries and the Mercer County Public Library. For aesthetic advice concerning the Shakers and their achievements, I thank Professor Nancy Coleman Wolsk of Transylvania University.

All of the documentary, newspaper, audio, and video material used in the preparation of the book has been placed in the library at Pleasant Hill, where anyone who wishes to consult it may do so.

Index

✤